FROM WHENCE WE CAME

AN ITALIAN SOJOURN

CHARLOTTE AMOREBELLO REMAKUS

221east

Hallstead, PA. USA

From Whence We Came:
An Italian Sojourn
CHARLOTTE AMOREBELLO REMAKUS

First Edition – February 2018
ISBN: 978-1975848033

All photos within this book were taken and modified by the author
unless otherwise noted. The poetry was written by the author
with the exception of the Ellis Island poem by Wallace Irwin.

This book is dedicated to my husband, children, and grandchildren

ACKNOWLEDGEMENTS

I am very grateful to all family members who helped bring this book to fruition. My husband Dr. Bernard Remakus, my son Dr. Christopher Remakus, my daughter Dr. Alexandra Novitsky, and my son Dr. Matthew Remakus, as well as their spouses, Dr. Mark Novitsky Jr. and Dr. Sanda Remakus provided verification of medical aspects of this book. My husband greatly helped with formatting, editing, publication, and production of the book cover.

My aunts Anna Mercuri Gallo and Marguerite Mecca Gibbons have provided me with much information and photos regarding the Mecca family. My cousin Dr. Anthony Mercuri Jr. gave me family stories and pictures.

My sisters Helen Lancia and Angela Lambert both accompanied me to Ellis Island and supplied me with photographs and stories. A special thank you goes to Angela Lambert who helped to research the history of the Mecca family.

My sister Lucy (Amorebello) Jason, my cousins Joseph Anthony Muracco, and Mickey (Juliano) Leonetti provided photos and stories regarding the Amorebello, Juliano, and Muracco families.

I am appreciative of pictures and stories provided by my cousins Tina Gittleman and Kathy Chrucky, who edited my manuscript and offered many helpful suggestions.

I tried to include photos of as many family members as I have obtained. If any photographs are missing it is because there were none available or publishing restrictions.

My cousin Doug Mecca from California added a considerable amount of information. Doug knew Italian and was able to access family accounts in that language. I met Doug on ancestry.com and we continue to share information.

Peter Mecca, Ph.D. contributed information and narratives to this endeavor, as well as my second cousins Angela McCarty and Peter Mecca Sr. Peter Mecca Sr. also showed us his scarf made from his brother Sal's burned parachute. Sal was a casualty of WWII.

My third cousin Joseph Galletti from France shared information about Salvatore Amorebello and family tree members. Joseph and I met on familysearch.org.

TABLE OF CONTENTS

CHAPTER 1 - INTRODUCTION

"The journey of a thousand miles begins with one step."
Li Bai - Chinese Poet, 8th c. Tang Dynasty

The geese are talking overhead on their flight south, and baby Charlotte sleeps. As Charlotte sleeps, it is a timeless moment for me. The cycles of nature repeat endlessly. The only importance in my world right now is that the geese fly, and baby Charlotte rests. The birth of a new generation has happened again and again, but for me, it is brand new.

The little hummingbirds fly and sip nectar, disappear to southern climes when colder weather arrives, and return. People have always moved for a better life. Hunter gatherers have followed herds for survival. All of life thrusts in a forward direction, and we will eventually soar beyond earth, following ancient stirrings calling our species ever onward despite the costs. Genetic inheritance will travel the expanses of space with them. Our species homo sapiens are irrepressible.

The importance of the preceding generations is that they have left an indelible mark on the present, and through their DNA, which this book will explore. People lived their lives, new families formed, new residences established, and a new generation of people existed. It is, in essence, our precious time on earth. How each of us came to be is a curious mix of people, places, history, climate, food sources, opportunity, steadfastness, and heredity. We should live this gift of life to the fullest, for ourselves, to honor our immigrant grandparents, and to ensure the futures of our grandchildren and beyond.

Our forebears could not envision the opportunities they forged for us by coming to a new world. To these beloved ancestors, our grandmothers and grandfathers, we owe our very being, our ambitions, our desires, and limitless futures. In this book I will follow the paths of my four grandparents and some of their descendants, from Italy in the early 20th century to my immediate family that exists today in the year 2017.

My new granddaughter Charlotte Kathleen (Baby Charlotte) is the fourth generation Charlotte that I know of directly in my family history. It is my name, a cousin's name, my paternal grandmother's name, and most likely her paternal grandmother, and very far back in time, I suppose. It was a family tradition among some Italians to name the first daughter after the child's paternal grandmother, and the second daughter after the maternal mother. A name became an heirloom, passed down through generations like a precious gem. Since I am my daughter's mother, I have received this amazing gift of having my little granddaughter named for me. A cycle repeats itself.

There seems to be an interest in genealogy these days as more and more people are scouring records to discover their ancestral past. One just has to check the internet to support this conclusion. Some pursue it with a passion, others are lukewarm, and some live vibrantly only in the present. Ralph Waldo Emerson said the present is our time to experience the universe in our way. I agree, but some Siren of myth is calling me, and I cannot ignore the call. What accounts for this burgeoning addiction to finding our roots in antiquity? For me, it was a desire to know more about people I never knew or knew only briefly. I am a semi-retired teacher now and have a lot of time for reflection and research.

At an earlier age, getting a college education at Marywood University, teaching at Dunmore High School, and raising my three children left little time for musings into the lives of my ancestors. I was like my mother then, a here and now person, involved with the generation at hand, and it was enough. Mom used to say that there was so much in today, "Grasp It." I believe that one should not live in bygone days, but knowing about that existence can add a dimension to life in the present.

My journey into my family's history was for me a detective story, and I wished to make sense of the family jigsaw puzzle. This journey began harmlessly enough in the summer of 2014 with a visit to my mother's grave at St. Catherine's Cemetery in Moscow, Pa. There were two grandmothers, three infants who barely had a chance to live, a grandfather who I consider a Renaissance man for his time, and my mother. Who were the unknown people entombed under the half-finished gray granite tombstone? Was the monument chosen to represent the shortened lives of those who repose so silently all these years?
Nearby were the graves of my mother's maternal grandparents and their only son, Anthony Towanda Paris, also known as Uncle "Cheesecake." This man I knew. He was a notorious and colorful member in my family tree, and I will have more to say about him in a later chapter. He was a lover, a soldier, and of all things, my babysitter.

I have always had an interest in other people's lives. I loved history from a young age. My mother once remarked that I "always had my nose in a book." I remembered poring over history books in my father's old bookcase, and at six years of age became enthralled with the North American Catholic martyrs and Saint Kateri Tekawitha, when I visited the Auriesville Shrine in upstate New York. The Catholic Church canonized Kateri as a saint recently.

In high school I became fascinated with the Civil War and cherished my first visit to the Gettysburg battlefield. I have always loved education in general and history, science, and psychology in particular. I have become a professional student, so you will see many disciplines incorporated into this book on family history.

My mother always asked me, "Why are you so interested in the past?" I think my answer now would be that besides my intense interest in people, I am also a latent family historian. My mother although, like Ralph Waldo Emerson, was a here and now "carpe diem" person knew quite a bit about her ancestral past. She believed in the limitless possibilities of every day, and I think she would have liked to start life over again just for the sheer joy of it. She had an uncanny sense of family relationships in our small town of Dunmore, Pennsylvania. She would say to me, Oh, you know Mrs. C on the Hill, who is related to Mr. B, who is the brother of Mr. G. Oh, I would say, "Yes, yes, I know who you mean." I just could not keep all of this straight, so I always said, "Sure I know."

I had a cursory knowledge of the beginnings of our family and listened intently to the stories told to me. Like so many other second or third generation children, I was wrapped up in my world in Dunmore, so I gave it little thought. I truly lived in the now, as if there were never any other time. I grew up in post- World War II where there was relative economic prosperity. Now that I am a septuagenarian with children and grandchildren, I decided to become an ancestral researcher and scour the sources available to see what I could find. I became so interested with the fun and drama of it all that I wished to share what I found with relatives and other interested family historians. I felt that all my time, research, and work should culminate in a physical account of how our family came to be. Whether or not this will enlighten me as to the person I am in a genealogical sense and aid in my future personal development remains to be seen. For now, I am just enjoying the literary journey.

So why do we write about our ancestry? Perhaps we wish to say we were here much like those who left the rock art in ancient caves. Chauvet Cave (The Cave of Forgotten Dreams) in southern France is filled with paintings dating back 30,000 years. It has one of the earliest known cave drawings. There are handprints made throughout the cave by someone with a crooked little finger.

This person with the cooked little finger was an artist of thousands of years ago who perhaps did some of the cave paintings. The deformed finger may have been due to an accident or other incident.

The artist with the crooked little finger found in the cave identified that particular artist in all of the other handprints in the cave.

It was his unique signature which indicated for all times that he was the person who left his handprint for others to see in the future. It is reminiscent of carving our initials on a tree. We were alive and we want the world to know it.

On the outskirts of Palermo, the Addaura Cave (Grotta dell' Addaura) is on the northeast side of Mount Pellegrino. Engravings date to 11,000 BCE. Because of these and other artifacts, we know that these ancient people existed.

Maybe this book is my way of imprinting my crooked little finger in the genealogical history of my family to remind them that I was here. Maybe it is a bid for a kind of immortality. All I know is that some unknown source propels me onward, and I want to tell my story. In a sense, it is every immigrant's story. It is about all of us who have people who made momentous decisions to bring us to where we are now.

My father's family came from San Cataldo, Caltanissetta, Sicily, Italy. Caltanissetta was originally a Moor settlement as the prefix Calta denotes. Calta means castle, therefore, a castle is in the area, but in disrepair. I will devote a section of my book to this part of the family, which includes my grandmother's parents, Frank and Carmella (Diliberto) Ingiamo. Later chapters will include my mother's father Dominick John Mecca Sr. and mother Angela Maria Paris. Great-Grandparents Peter and Serafina Paris and their son Anthony Towanda Paris have their place in this narrative. Anthony T. Paris, who was called to duty for the Mexican Expedition to capture Pancho Villa in the early 1900s, was my babysitter at a later time.

My mother has an important place in this story as she was my first love, and through her and her maternal line, I will trace my mtDNA (mitochondrial DNA), which has implications dating thousands of years ago. Through it, we can trace our maternal migratory pattern to our final place of origin (Sicily and Southern Italy). In fact, I am awaiting the results of this study which I will include later.

My paternal grandfather Luigi Amorebello was in his thirties when he sailed into New York. I often wonder when the idea came to him to sail to America and why. They were in survival mode, and I doubt they gave much thought to future generations beyond their immediate family. Somehow our genes forge onward.

My maternal grandfather came from Avigliano, Potenza, Basilicata, Italy. He was a very young child when he arrived in Dunmore, Pennsylvania with his family. He was resourceful and accomplished many things in his short life.

Although I will never know the coming generations beyond my three young granddaughters and grandson, I hope we leave them a better world or maybe worlds, as we venture beyond earth.

Steven Hawking the famed cosmologist suggests that we must move humans beyond earth so that our extinction does not occur. It is like saying that we should not put our collective DNA into one basket.

I am sure Grandfather Luigi was not thinking about generations into the future. There was too much at stake at that time, more pressing issues than speculating about the far distant future. He could never have known that in 2017, he would have two Asian/Italian/Polish great- great grandchildren in his line in years to come, or that those children's grandfather and family immigrated to America (Philadelphia) to escape from Cambodia in the 1970s.

He could not know that two beautiful little great-great granddaughters in the 21st century would be living in Pennsylvania, so far away from the Sicily of their ancestors.

Luigi and Cologera Amorebello had a great-great-great grandchild added to their family tree. Their great-great grandson Matthew Jason and his wife Lindsay had a son, Calvin Duke Matthew, October 2016. My sister Lucy is a great-grandmother now. Life continues.

As I write this book, I am wondering about onomatology or the source of my particular families' surnames. Historically in Sicily last names were not adopted until the mid -15th century. One can trace their lineage in Sicily back to about this date because the government kept genealogical records. I would be happy to research to about 1800. In Sicily the genealogical records are intact. Surnames reflected where you lived, what your occupation was, or it may have reflected a character or physical trait. "Amorebello" means "beautiful love," so perhaps there was a dashing conqueror in the family's past after all. Women in Sicily tended to keep their maiden names; this was reflected in the fact that ship's manifests list the woman's maiden name. This was valuable in determining relationships.

Throughout the text there might be different spellings of family names. Some variations in names had to do with family preferences or spelling errors. Sister Lucy and I always used "Amorebello" in school, so perhaps the change in spelling occurred at that time.

The "Mecca" surname means "one who lived near a noisy venue," as a marketplace. There are 400 households with the name Mecca in the United States.

I would like to include anecdotal records of lives lived whenever possible. As ancestors recede into the past, stories will become more and more difficult to retrieve, and I will have to speculate based on the historical events of those times. I do have photos, however, of progenitors I never knew, and perhaps they will inspire some conjectures on appearance alone. My last chapter will include photos of family members and I hope this will add to the enjoyment of my readers.

My interest in writing this book is to trace my lineage regarding four grandparents, their offspring, how they arrived in this country, how they lived, and their legacy. I would like to explore the reasons which might have contributed to their immigration, and what they endured to arrive in Dunmore, Pennsylvania. I would like to present a historical perspective as to the times my ancestors lived, as well as delving into diseases that influenced my family's history and the transfer of their DNA, which the succeeding generations have inherited.

When I decided to embark on this journey into the past, I already had quite a few names, places, and stories gathered from oral histories and photographs. I had a baseline from which to work. There are still some relatives alive on both sides, the oldest being 93 years of age, whom I may still consult. Once I began musing as to who lay in the graves of my immediate ancestors at various nearby cemeteries, I began my research in earnest. Bringing the dead to life again for my relatives and readers became an overriding desire, and I wanted to be sure that it was an accurate story of my four families.

Finally, I hope this information will be of interest to my family and the general reader, and perhaps help others to delve into their own ancestral stories.

CHAPTER 2 – THE PLAN FOR MY RESEARCH

"One lives as long as he is remembered." Russian Proverb

This research has taken me more than three years. Many sites on ancestry.com were perused, many books and articles were read, and many videos and documentaries were consulted. Visits were made to Ellis Island and cemeteries where my progenitors were buried.

I took a creative writing short course with Anne Vitale through the Montrose Adult School. This course helped me with examining all aspects of my writing. One of Anne's tenets was to "kill the baby." By this she meant that the writer may wish to include things that do not totally fit with the theme of the book. In my exuberance to produce this manuscript, I violated the rule.

I will stop at the juncture of my three sisters and myself, as well as my spouse and three children. This way my book will be a story in progress, and current descendants and those in the future can add to the story.

I subscribed to Ancestry.com so I could look up pertinent records for my research. Ancestry.com has been an invaluable aid. I studied Ellis Island's ships' manifests, and found a virtual tour of Ellis Island, which added a lot of substance to the immigrants' experience. A visit was planned in conjunction with the writing of this book to personally experience what it was like to be an immigrant in the early 20th century.

YouTube had many videos on what transpired at Ellis Island, and there was a plethora of books on the subject, so it was not difficult to learn even more about this period in history.

I consulted the Mormon Organization-Family Search (familysearch.org) which promotes the study of one's forebears, and is free for anyone who is researching their ancestry. The Granite Mountain Records Vault is in Utah.

The Church of Jesus Christ of the Latter Days Saints began in the 1950s. The Mormons have millions of personal records stored behind a fourteen-ton steel door. In the event of a nuclear explosion, it will be sealed in. This religious group has more than 3400 Family History Centers in the world and will help anyone who wishes to find out more about his progenitors.

Some family members provided me with stories and photographs, previously unknown to me. These stories and photos are in the book.

Other researchers involved in searching for information on mutual ancestors have helped me in this quest. I have a hard copy of an interview of our first cousins (Anna and Mary) from Sherwood Avenue, Dunmore, Pa., who knew a lot about the family history on the Mecca side. My cousins were the first generation of Americans. My sister Angela Lambert conducted this research.

According to Angela, much of this information our ninety-four -year old Great-Aunt Angelina provided. This interview took place in the 1960s. Angelina was our maternal grandfather's older sister, who accompanied him and the family to New York in 1901.

Dominick's other sister was Maria Giuseppe (Aunt Josephine) who married Dominick Mecca and lived on Walnut Street. Grandfather's brother Bill was married and lived on Smith Street.

Great-Grandfather Angelo Mecca was born on January 28, 1847 at twelve noon in Avigliano, Potenza, Basilicata, Italy. Great- Grandfather was baptized on January 29, 1847 at San Carmines.

Angelo was the son of our great-great grandfather Vincenzo Maria (1811-1883) who was a grain miller and managed the farm. Angelo's mother was Carminella Colangelo (1815-1903). Angelo had several other siblings, but some did not survive infancy.

Vincenzo Maria's father was also named Angelo, our great-great-great grandfather (b. before 1790) and Vincenzo's mother was Maria.

The father of Angelo (b. before 1790) was known as Sebastiano Mecca, our great-great-great-great grandfather (b. before 1770) and Angelo's mother was Rosa Maria. This was as far as we could go for this Mecca family.

Landowners were considered to be upper middle class in Italy at this time. The farm had a flour mill, vineyards, olive orchards, and grain crops, as well as sheep and goats. Great-Grandfather Angelo drank goat's milk from his hat when working in the fields. Great-Grandfather wore gold earrings to enhance his eyesight, which was common practice.

When Angelo (b.1847) was older he managed the farm, and once he was married the parents moved out but lived nearby.

Angelo was married four times. The parents arranged each marriage. Two of his wives died in childbirth. His second wife Filomena Romano died at twenty-four years of age in 1868. The name of his first wife was not known. Angelo (1847-1923) married his third wife on March 30, 1868. Her name was Rosa Maria Rinaldi (1847-1882). Rosa Maria's parents were Domenico Antonio Rinaldi (b.1829) and Angela Maria Trotta (b.1829). Angelo and Rosa Maria had two children Vito Vincenzo (b.1869) and Mary (b. before 1875). Rosa Maria died September 28, 1882.

Great-Grandfather Angelo married his fourth wife Anna Maria Mecca on June 6, 1883 before Andrea Claps, a priest. Anna Maria was the daughter of Vito Mecca (1818-1883) and Angela Tolle (b.1821). Angelo and Anna Maria had four children: Angelina, Josephine, William, and Dominick John (our grandfather).

The children did not go to school when they lived in Avigliano but instead worked on the farm. Aunt Angelina remembered working in the fields, canning food, and making wine.

Vito Vincenzo (James) Mecca and his wife Carmela (Rinaldi) Mecca arrived in Dunmore, Pa. in c. 1892 and sent for the rest of the family (father Angelo, step-mother Anna Maria, half-siblings: Angelina, Josephine, William, and Dominick John) in March, 1901.

Mary stayed in Italy, was married, kept the farm, and eventually her family immigrated to Canada. Our great-great grandparent Vincenzo Maria died in 1883 and his wife Carminella (Colangelo) Mecca remained in Italy. Carminella died in 1903.

When the Mecca family arrived in Dunmore in 1901 they bought a house on Smith Street. Angelo worked at the Number 5 Breaker, while Anna Maria took care of the children. There was no electricity in the home only kerosene lamps. They had to use outhouses.

Only the boys, William and Dominick, were allowed to receive an education. Aunt Angelina said, "My brothers tried to help me with English and writing, but my father would not allow it." "He said it would corrupt me and give me bad ideas, and I might write to boys." Father Angelo made all the decisions.

Aunt Angelina and her sister Aunt Jessie (Josephine) washed clothes, baked bread, picked coal, gathered berries, and cared for the younger children. Adults masticated food before feeding it to the babies. It was their version of making baby food. The brothers went to school but also picked slate. The children who picked slate from coal were known as "breaker boys."

The girls married early, Angelina at sixteen years of age, and Josephine at seventeen. William married at twenty-two and Dominick at nineteen. Children were married young to help offset the financial burden to a family. The girls' dowry included money, and hope chests, which contained household items such as sheets, quilts, and dish towels.

William worked for the Delaware and Western Railroad after he graduated from high school. William inherited everything as he was the oldest son of Angelo's marriage with Anna Maria.

Apparently, inheritance by the oldest son was common practice for some families in Italy known as primogenitor. Younger sons often entered the priesthood. Dominick was not happy with the inheritance decision, and a rift occurred between the brothers. Angelo and Anna Maria lived with William and his family most of their lives.

Dominick finished high school and went on to Saint Thomas College (now the University of Scranton). He became interested in pharmacy and continued his education at Temple University in Philadelphia, Pa. He became a pharmacist and opened his drugstore in Dunmore. As he was already married, he had no financial support from his parents.

Grandfather's family lived on Willow Street and then moved to the home on Chestnut Street. A fire destroyed this home in February 1981. The building was originally a general store with a warehouse upstairs. Dominick converted it to a drugstore on the first floor, and apartments on the second and third floors.

There was also an A& P store (American chain grocery store that ceased operations in November 2015, after 156 years of business) and a barber shop. I spent my early childhood in this home on Chestnut Street, and I remembered the large spacious rooms with the turn of the century furniture, the huge back porch where the family spent summer days, and my bedroom where I watched the street light glowing while trying to fall asleep.

Two early memories at this home which upset my mother were when the male cousins, who hung around our house, held me over the balcony and pretended to drop me. I remembered screaming, and my mother scolding them. It was pretty high up. The other memory was teasingly being locked in the mailbox outside the drugstore by the mischievous cousins who pretended not to let me out. I remembered yelling and kicking the mailbox. Growing up tough was what it was all about apparently.

Throughout my childhood, my mother often told me family stories, which I will share as I go along. Of particular interest was my mother's parrot, Polly, which woke her up every morning saying, "Sarah, Get up for school." This pet used to fly around my grandfather's pharmacy. The poor parrot met his demise when he flew headlong into a glass window. Notice the sign in the background of following photo which reads "Repeal Dry Law."

My mother and her parrot, Polly

According to the National Constitution Center, the 18th Amendment went into effect on January 17, 1920 which prohibited the making or selling of alcohol. The Prohibitionists hoped to raise the nation's physical and moral health. However, an increase in crime resulted.

The "wets" fought back successfully, and the ratification of the 21st Amendment restored the use of alcohol in America in 1933. A family story suggested that one of my great aunts produced the banned alcohol in a still in her bathroom. She was probably one of many "bootleggers" in the small town of Dunmore.

On another note, I tried to behave as much as possible because I did not want to "be sold to the gypsies." Where that saying came from I may never know, but will try to research it. I think it worked as a great behavioral management tool. In retrospect, I think I might have seen one of those "gypsies." He was an organ grinder with a little brown monkey dressed in a red suit with embroidered gold trim, and matching hat. We children were all amused to see the organ grinder appear on the sidewalk and play his music, as the monkey danced and performed many cute antics. It was better than what I think a Punch and Judy show might have been like in England, or maybe the Italian Marionettes (Opera dei Pupi) who entertained and amused audiences in Italy. I liked this particular "gypsy" and his little monkey. However, I did not want to be a part this "gypsy" family.

Organ grinders dated back 300 years. When the Italian immigrants came to New York, some Italian men supported their families by playing the organ on street corners, while their little Capuchin monkey, dressed in his little suit, performed his antics. Because of his opposable thumb, the little monkey was able to hold a cup and collect the coins from the audience.

Another behavioral management technique was the challenge, "What will they say?" I was always curious as to who the "they" were and asked my mother. She looked at me and had to give that a second thought herself. To this day, I am still interested in who the "they "were. I think maybe they were researchers with all kinds of evidence-based studies and had to be taken seriously. In my childhood it stopped me dead in my tracks, as did the gypsy story.

Although the organ grinder was not a gypsy, I did have the opportunity to befriend real gypsies, who were fortune tellers. We both worked at the now defunct Rocky Glen Amusement Park in Moosic, Pa. I remembered them as very kind people. My mother would translate written letters for them as the gypsies could not read nor write.

The elusive "they," actually, it is a photo of my Grandmother Calogero Amorebello's 90th birthday celebration. The author is third row, third person from the left. My mother is second row, the first person from the left. My sister Angela Lambert is in the first row, the first person from the left.

The cousins discuss aspects of the Amorebello, Juliano, and Muracco families. Left to right: Vincent Jason, Joseph A. Muracco, Susan Muracco, Mickey (Juliano) Leonetti, Lucy (Amorebello) Jason

Since I included a background of historical information regarding the time periods during which my ancestors lived, I consulted books and articles on the history, both printed and online websites, and will mention some of these sources in the main body of my work as I progress. The Black Death which reached Messina, Sicily, Italy first in its expansion through the rest of Europe was of interest. Although not completely eradicated in the present day, and outbreaks do occur, it is treatable with antibiotics.

There will be an inclusion of some current studies in DNA, and a discussion of what it suggested for me. Recently I had my autosomal DNA and mitochondrial DNA tested and will share the results. The deciphering of DNA is a new and fascinating study of the human genome which personalizes it for the average person. Using this research, we can trace our ancestry to a scientific Adam and a scientific Eve, and seven branches of women from her. I will briefly touch on this research in a later chapter and challenge you to think about which of the seven daughters of Eve you think you might have a link. I will let you know all about my link and what that meant for me.

CHAPTER 3 – HISTORICAL PERSPECTIVES

"One who is ignorant of what happened before his birth will always be a child."
Cicero

Here is a short history of Sicily. It is not a historical narrative per se. I felt it important to generalize aspects of the island to provide a setting for the lives of my ancestors. The first people entered Sicily via the Straits of Messina into the northeast roughly 20,000 years ago. There was another hypothesis that suggested that they came from Africa. The current data, however, favored the Straits of Messina route. A hominid skull called the "girl of Mandrascava" was found near Agrigento, Sicily. The skull is thought to be 500,000 years old. This finding of the remains just puts into perspective how old hominid existence might be on the island.

From these early beginnings, Sicilians are descended from at least twelve different civilizations. They came from Sicilian, Phoenicians, Greeks, Carthaginians, Romans, Byzantine Greeks, Saracen Arabs, Normans, Longobards, Goths, Angevin French, Aragonese and Spanish, as well as from Albanians who appeared in the sixteenth century. The languages spoken by the early Sicilians were like Phoenician and Greek. The Island was at the crossroads of Africa, Europe, and Asia. It became a very strategic military objective. Sicily has been invaded and conquered many times over. It was a multicultural society very early in its history.

The people of Trinicaria as the Greeks called Sicily have had to adapt to different conquerors over most of their history. According to Louis Mendola in his book *"Sicilian Genealogy and Heraldry"* he stated the Elymians arrived 1300 BC (BCE), Phoenicians and Greeks 750 BC, Carthaginians 500 BC, Romans 227 BC, Jews 146 BC, Vandals AD (CE) 440, and Goths 476.

Byzantine Greeks entered 535, Longobard incursions 568, Arabs and Berbers 827, Normans and Lombards 1061, Swabians (Germans) 1194, Angevins (French) 1266, Aragonese (later Spanish) 1282, Albanian refugees 1470.

Some aspects of history were pivotal in the island's development. The French ruled Sicily for a short time. Naples was the capital. After the Vespers War, the term "Two Sicilies" was used as Charles of Anjou (French) in Palermo and Peter of Aragon (Spanish) both claimed the throne.

The French were ousted in 1282 (the War of the Sicilian Vespers). A French soldier insulted a Sicilian woman as she was returning from church on Easter Monday vespers, and all chaos broke out. The French were defeated, and the populace nearly massacred all the French in Sicily.

Even if you were Sicilian and married to someone French, you did not escape retribution. The French were not able to pronounce the word "ciciri", which are chickpeas or garbanzo beans, and thus were quickly identified and slaughtered. Others escaped death and were deported.

Go to *Howtopronounce.com* if you would like to know how to say "ciciri".

Where was our family at this time, I wonder? Did they take part in the uprising? Though I will never know, it is interesting to speculate.

After the French, Sicily was offered to Peter of Aragon (Spanish). The Aragon fleet arrived and the Island was ruled by Spain for 500 years (1282-1700s). Peace and prosperity reigned during this time until the Spanish Inquisition (1492). During the Inquisition, the Jews had to convert to Catholicism or were deported.

Albanian refugees arrived (c.1493) in Sicily because of Turkish invasions of the Balkans. By 1500, there were over a thousand Albanian families, and many thousands of Sicilians today can trace their ancestry to Albania.

The advent of the Normans, who preceded the French and Spanish in 1066, was of interest because of what they did for Sicily. At this time The Kingdom of Sicily south of Rome was referred to as The Kingdom (Regnum). It included Sicily and most of the peninsula of southern Italy. The Normans were of Viking descent, came to Sicily in 1061 and found the Arabs and Greeks living in harmony. The Arabs had built a sophisticated society and brought in lemon, oranges, dates, and sugar cane.

The Arabs cultivated mulberries for the silk industry, and their harems increased the population of Sicily considerably. Palermo was one of the most splendid cities of the world under Arab rule.

The Normans continued to live in peace with the incumbent populations and adopted the rich Arab culture. This new society was a model of tolerance and respect.

The two Golden Ages in Sicily lasted less than 200 years. The golden age of the Normans was from 1072-1194. The second golden age was under Frederick II who wore the crown from 1198-1250. This relative calm disintegrated near the end of the 13th century.

During the Norman rule, John Julius Norwich (*The Kingdom in the Sun, 1970*) said, "Norman Sicily stood forth in Europe-and indeed the whole bigoted medieval world-as an example of tolerance and enlightenment, a lesson in the respect that every man should feel toward those whose blood and beliefs happen to differ from his own."

It is noteworthy to my ancestors and their descendants that Caltanissetta was captured by Count Roger in 1068, and presented to his son King Roger ll. I am wondering what effect this might have had on the families of our ancestry. Did the Norman invaders freely marry the Sicilians? Could we have Norman ancestors? We had some light-skinned, blue-eyed, red hair descendants, which might suggest some "Normanna" (Normans) were present in our genes. By contrast dark-haired beauties were referred to as "Mora" (Moors).

The manorial or feudal was prominent in Sicily during Norman times. A manor consisted of a small village built around a tower attached to an insulated courtyard. It was essentially a large rural estate made up of many farms rented to tenants. The landlord who managed the lands lived in a nearby town.

The earliest barons, in exchange for the land, owed the king military time of just over one month a year.

Until about 1266, most people in Sicily had freedom, but in court, the feudal lord had the final say.   At a later date, commoners purchased land, but the lord of the manor dictated the land use. Tax records indicated that back to the 15th century many peasants owned their land, but they had to have permits for which they paid to hunt, fish, plant trees, or add anything to their land holdings. Feudalism ended in 1812.

In the 18th and 19th centuries, most Sicilian families owned their homes and maybe a plot of land. Our ancestor Luigi Amorebello born in 1796 perhaps lived in his own home on a plot of land with his family. Luigi's parents lived at the time of the American Revolution. Did they have knowledge of what was going on in the rest of the world? Or did they just go about the business of eking out a living on the less than fertile land?

By 1867 (after the unification of Italy in 1861), Church holdings were auctioned off and in 1949 and 1950 what remained of the large estates were limited. The wealthy owned parcels of land and the peasant farmers managed the remaining lots.

Our grandfather Luigi Amorebello (1875-1959) would have been born after the unification of Italy in 1861. His parents Vincenzo and Luisa would have lived in the midst of that turmoil and perhaps even taken part. I wonder if they saw this as a good thing for Sicily at that time, or if the repercussions further disillusioned the already down-trodden Sicilians.

After the Normans, the crown passed to the Germans (Swabians). The Swabian (German) rule was harsh. The Golden Age of Sicily had ended. Ferdinando combined Sicily and Neapolitan territories into the two Sicilies in 1816 (The Kingdom of the Two Sicilies). Previous to this, there were the unofficial "two Sicilies" because Charles of Aragon (French) and Peter of Aragon (Spanish) both claimed the Sicilian crown.

The Kingdom of the Two Sicilies (Naples and Sicily reunited in 1816) and lasted until Italian Unification in 1861.

At that period, literacy throughout Italy was only 20%. That changed with the unification of Italy in 1861.

In 1877, the time of Cologera Ingiamo's birth (my paternal grandmother) primary education up to the third grade was compulsory in unified Italy.

In 1860, Garibaldi and his 1000 "red shirts" captured Sicily and then southern Italy in the name of King Victor Emmanuel II. Thousands joined in the uprising.

In 1861, Garibaldi (1807-1882) freed the Italians from foreign rule. This invasion was not Garibaldi's first attempt at throwing off unwanted governments. He knew guerilla warfare and in 1848 fought to throw off the rule of Austria in Italy. It failed. Garibaldi learned much in the intervening years and was successful finally in 1861.

There were riots and opposition to the new government under King Victor ll.

Sicily and southern Italy were repressed and thousands of people were executed, made prisoner, or deported.

In 1866, there was an uprising in Palermo. The city was bombed and the insurgents executed.

In 1894, the organization of Sicilian Workers Leagues led to more government control.

In 1860, Vincenzo Amorebello my paternal great-grandfather (about seventeen years old at that time) was living in San Cataldo, as well as Francesco Ingiamo (Grandmother's father) who was about the same age. These great-grandfathers would have been of age to join the rebellion and fight for the unification of Italy. I wonder if they took part in this momentous time in Sicily.

Did my ancestors support the Unification, or were they in the resistance movement? Did they fight in any of the battles? It was written that in some cases the average Sicilian really did not care. They were more interested in earning a living, than in who ruled the country. It will probably never be known what my ancestors' involvement might have been, but they were there during this critical period in Italian history. At the time of Italian Unification, Abraham Lincoln was President of the United States, and the Queen of England was Queen Victoria.

In 1920, Benito Mussolini led a Fascist dictatorship. His alliance with Nazi Germany was disastrous for Italy. Germany and Italy were defeated by the Allies.

Postwar Italy

The Italian monarchy existed for a short time. It was replaced in 1946 by a democratic republic. Italy was a charter member of NATO and the European Economic Community.

I will stop at this point in Italian history as my ancestors were permanently living in America. My grandparents never returned to Italy.

The plague came to Sicily in 1347. I do not know which ancestors would have been alive at this point, but they somehow survived. Why some people did not come down with the plague has to do with our DNA.

Some people have more resistant immune systems because of their genes. Or maybe they were subjected to a less virulent strain of the plague and did not get the disease. If they were naturally resistant, they were thought to have the CCR5 (delta) 32 gene. This particular gene gave resistance to small pox and human immune deficiency virus (HIV).

Recent studies, however, published in the Proceedings for the National Academy of Science (Feb. 18, 2014) took Immune cells from people with the variant TLR genes and mixed them with Yersinia pestis (Black Plague microbes).

TLR variants had an immune response. It may be this variant rather than CCR5 (delta) 32 that conferred the immunity. Those fortunate individuals passed on these genes to future generations.

I believe my ancestors must have had this gene variant and survived those dreadful times, or else they had excellent immune systems. Since they were inland from ground zero at Messina, perhaps the plague bacteria were less innocuous. Of course, we can be tested genetically to see if we have this variant (TLR), but the DNA tests I took did not include this type of result.

In the case of the Amorebello and Ingiamo ancestors, they would most likely have been in the center of Sicily (Caltanissetta) and in a sense quarantined from what was happening in Messina.

The Black Death spread throughout Europe in the middle of the 14th century. It was most likely carried from Central Asia by trading routes, and then to coast ports by merchant ships. The plague ships arrived in Messina, Sicily in the autumn of 1347. When the inspectors boarded the ships, they found sick and dying sailors. The ships were instructed to depart, but it was too late. The plague had spread to Europe. From 1347-53 about 25 million people succumbed. Some believed it was the end of the world. 'How many valiant men, how many fair ladies, breakfasted with their kinsfolk and that same night supped with their ancestors in the other world.' (Giovanni Boccaccio 1313-1375)

The black rat (Rattus rattus) transmits Yersinia pestis (a gram-negative bacterium) through flea bites. "Whether you die or not depends on how fast and efficiently your immune system reacts to the infection. Bacteria proliferate rapidly, and the body is overrun in a matter of hours. Toxins produced caused disseminated intravascular coagulation," says Susan Lance, spokeswoman for the Centers for Disease Control

Division of Vector Infectious Diseases. "You get gangrene in your extremities because the blood is clotted in the little capillaries and it turns black."

Hard swollen buboes appeared on the body near where the flea has bitten. The symptoms of the plague were black boils that oozed blood and pus, fever, chills vomiting, diarrhea, aches, and pains. Physicians tried bloodletting, lancing the boils using aromatic herbs, and washing the afflicted in rosewater or vinegar. The plague affected cows, sheep, goats, pigs, and chickens. The citizens killed stray dogs and cats. Strangely, no one yet suspected the rats, although the rodents were dead as well. Bodies were piled high in the streets, or tossed onto rafts and allowed to drift out to sea.

The plague could also enter the lungs and could then be passed on to the next person. It is called pneumonic plague at this stage. Septicemic plague was the most virulent. The body was covered in black sores, due to the hemorrhaging and has 100% mortality. Those that recovered are immune for life. Panic ensued, and those that were able fled the cities for the countryside. Quarantine was the only thing that worked, and by 1351 the plague had disappeared.

However, the plague reappeared periodically in Europe and elsewhere with dire consequences. Petrarch remarked: 'Is it possible that posterity can believe these things? For we, who have seen them, can hardly believe them.' The gravediggers threw caution to the wind, charged exorbitant prices to bury the dead, and then partied all night. They probably felt they had nothing to lose as most people expected to die.

Peasants were in short supply, and they demanded higher pay and better working conditions.

It is interesting that because of the plague, macabre art became very popular in the 15th and 16th centuries.

The plague still exists, and there are periodic outbreaks. There are about 180 deaths per year mostly in Africa. Colorado in the U.S. has also reported cases. Today plague is treated with antibiotics.

Francesco Ingiamo (1844-1911)   Frank Amorebello (1914-1946)

My father (right) resembles his grandfather Francesco.

CHAPTER 4 – ELLIS ISLAND

*"Ellis Island is one of the greatest human nature offices in the world;
not a week passes without its comedies as well as tragedies."
William Williams, Ellis Island Commissioner 1912.*

*"What the son wishes to forget, the grandson wishes to remember."
Marcus Lee Hansen 1938.*

Ellis Island to me conjured up ideas of freedom, new opportunities, and like Daedalus and his wings of wax, an escape from somewhere less perfect. I always envisioned coming to Ellis Island as a glorious experience for the immigrants. My heart warmed to the photos or video clips of the ships passing the Statue of Liberty, and the new life that awaited those ocean voyagers. I read the beautiful poem by Emma Lazarus, written in 1883, which was inscribed at the base of Lady Liberty. "Give me your tired, your poor, your huddled masses yearning to breathe free, the wretched refuse of your teeming shore. Send these, the homeless, tempest-tossed to me; I lift my lamp beside the golden door."

I was proud to be an American, who welcomed all those downtrodden by sheer life circumstances. I was too uninformed. There was much more to the story than I could ever think possible. There were problems with immigration in the past as there are today. I was stunned to discover that there were divided camps in the United States regarding the wave of the massive immigration from the old world.

This poem by Wallace Irwin, *Ellis Island's Problems*, sums up what some of the nation were thinking about the huddled masses. There were Americans who wanted the masses to continue to huddle on their shores in Europe and not come to America.

*Down the greasy gang-plank
See the motley pack
Nothing in the pocketbook
Tatters on the back*

> *Pauper, cripple, criminal*
> *Halt and blind and slow*
> *Has Uncle Sammy room enough*
> *To give them all a show*
>
> *Crime, disease, and wretchedness*
> *Of a hundred lands*
> *All of the world's incompetence*
> *Dumped upon our hands*

There were many reasons for this rush to leave their homelands. There was the potato famine in Ireland, poverty in Italy, Germans escaping economic upheaval and political unrest, Jews fleeing the pogroms in Europe, and universal reasons of why people left their homelands.

Ellis Island had a history of its own, long before the mass immigration to the island in the early 1900s. In the early 1600s, the Mohegan Indians called it Gull Island. A Dutch man, Michael Paauw named it Oyster Island because of the abundance of shellfish. In the mid-1700s, Mr. Ellis built a tavern, and the state of New York bought it when Mr. Ellis died.

During the war of 1812, it was a military fort, and during the civil war, it was used as a munitions arsenal for the Union Army. After the Civil War, it replaced the immigration station at Castle Garden which closed in 1890. Today Castle Garden is Castle Clinton where tickets are purchased to visit Ellis Island and the Statue of Liberty. In the early 19th-century pirate hangings took place on Ellis Island, then known as Gibbets Island. The last hanging took place on Liberty Island, where the base of the Statue of Liberty now stands. New Yorkers would come out in boats on the Hudson River to witness the hangings.

The Homestead Act of 1862, which gave land to the American West, encouraged Europeans to immigrate. By 1882, restrictions were placed on prostitutes, criminals, lunatics, and idiots from entering the country. The Chinese Exclusion Act was passed in 1882. In 50 years more than 12 million people passed through Ellis Island, and between 1840 and 1920 was the greatest migration in human history, when almost 40 million people came to America.

There was a fire in 1897; no one was killed. A new fireproof facility was built in 1902. Landfill increased the size of Ellis Island, and Island Two was the hospital administration and contagious diseases ward. Island Three held the psychiatric ward. Today it is the Ellis Island Immigration Museum, and is part of the Statue of Liberty National Monument supervised by the National Parks Service.

The Author and Helen Lancia

The Author and Angela Lambert

My two sisters and I journeyed to NYC and Ellis Island (2014) to experience what it was like to arrive at the Island as an immigrant. As we ferried across the Hudson to the National Park, I tried to imagine what the traveler felt when coming to America for the first time. Was it hope, exhilaration, fear?

The Great Hall at Ellis Island was what impressed you, and you could almost imagine the throngs of immigrants waiting to be "processed." Doctors at Ellis Island had a dual role. They were supposed to do a quick review of those passing by, and had to mark those with chalk on their clothing for further examination. Contagious diseases meant exclusion, and immigrants were sent back to their home ports.

Grandfather had come over as steerage. It was called steerage because that is where the steerage mechanisms of previously used sailing ships were kept. It cost $35 to $46 to sail over, and involved about two week's time. The steerage of the ship could hold two thousand passengers and was a lucrative venture for steamship owners. Steerage was unsanitary and lacked privacy. The occupants slept in metal bunks. Before 1910, passengers sat on deck or below and ate meals from a tin mess kit.

Grandfather was in his 30s when he sailed into New York. I wonder when the idea came to him to sail to America and why. Was it the poverty; the political circumstances? How did he arrive at the point of embarkation in Palermo? Was he alone or did he travel with others? On board ship where did he sleep, what did he eat, whom did he talk to, and what did he think?

The Passenger Record obtained from Ellis Island reads - Name: Luigi Amoribello, Ethnicity Italian Residence San Cataldo, Italy, Date of Arrival: 12 Nov 1907, Age on Arrival 32, Gender M, Marital Status M, Ship of Travel: Madonna, Port of Departure: Naples, Compania, Italy.

In 1907, when Grandfather Luigi arrived on the Madonna 1.25 million immigrants came that year. This was a record not to be broken for the next eighty years. If everything was in order and health was good, the inspection took 3-5 hours. However, if there were any impediments you were sent back (2 % were excluded). For some people, this place was called the Island of Tears. If a child was 12 years of age, he was sent back alone. If the child was under 12 years, one parent had to go back with him.

There was some humor as you might expect. Some immigrants were coached by others, who had been through the experience, cheat sheets, so to speak. The travelers had to show the inspectors that they had between $18 and $25 to enter the U.S. Cleverly, the same $25 was passed from immigrant to immigrant.

A system of using chalk on clothing designated a person may have a disability, which was a hindrance for admittance to the U.S.

If an immigrant were in need of further examination, a letter was written in chalk on his clothing. For example, an X high up on the shoulder would mean a mental defect; an X further down, a disease or deformity. Pg designated pregnancy and Ct an eye disease.

The resourceful passengers would either wipe off the marks of chalk or turn their coats inside out to avoid further evaluation.

Grandfather in 1907 would have ferried over to Ellis Island from the port of New York. On his clothing would be a tag with his manifest number. Grandfather next had a medical exam. His hair, face, neck, and hands were examined.

Grandfather would have been asked 29 questions, for example, what is your occupation, how much money do you have on you, where did you come from, where are you going, who is at home in your town of origin, what is your religion, and whom are you going to meet? Grandfather would have had an eye exam, as trachoma (a contagious eye disease that could cause blindness, and possibly death was a reason for exclusion). A button hook was used to invert the upper eyelid and look for inflammation or disease. It was reported to be somewhat painful. The doctors used the same hook for each, and infection surely had to spread.

Since psychological testing and mental examination were not instituted until 1917, Grandfather missed this aspect of screening. This was interesting to me as a former school psychologist. We were able to examine firsthand the puzzle that the immigrants were asked to assemble. The task was to help ascertain their mental status.

A little girl of about ten years of age worked on the problem the day we visited and finally did get it right. The child did take some time to complete the task. The puzzles I had my students assemble during psychological testing were much easier by comparison. My test puzzles had pictures.

It was not an easy problem, especially for those who had never experienced putting a puzzle together. *"Golden Door" 2006*, an Italian movie depicting immigrant arrival at Ellis Island c. 1917 is an excellent portrayal of what the detainees for further examination experienced. The father of the family was asked to put the puzzle together. Instead, he constructed a house and fenced yard from the pieces. He seemed pleased with himself for a job well done, and looked to his examiner for approval. The task was clear to him that he was expected to construct a three-dimensional house out of the puzzle pieces.

One saw the disparity between what the average immigrant knew, and his limited exposure to such things. Conversely, a fellow female passenger, English and very literate, put the puzzle together correctly in a matter of minutes. It was hard to construct culture-free bias in psychological testing.

Fortunately, only those people detained for further evaluation had additional testing and more detailed medical examinations. What Grandfather did next is not known, but eventually, he ended up in Dunmore, Pa. Lucy Jason (my sister) believed he was met by his sponsor who vouched for him (chain migration) and met him in New York. Grandfather probably lived in Dunmore with his sponsor initially.

Grandmother Calogera (Ingiamo) Amorebello, and her two children, James (Vincenzo) and Louisa, arrived in New York (1908) on the Madonna and would have experienced the physical examination and questions as well. Perhaps Grandfather met his young family at the "kissing post" before beginning their new lives in America. The "kissing post" was located outside the Registry room where people met up with their relatives. My grandparents went to live in Dunmore, Pa. with their young family, and Grandmother and Grandfather remained there the rest of their long lives.

One-third of the American population can trace their ancestry to Ellis Island. Not all immigrants remained in America. Some came to earn money and return to their families in Europe.

During and following World War II, 6800 Japanese, Germans, and Italians, who were thought to be enemies of the U.S., were held at Ellis Island. When the war ended in 1945 President Truman ordered those aliens, deemed dangerous, to be deported.

CHAPTER 5 –

GRANDFATHER AND GRANDMOTHER AMOREBELLO

"La familia e la patria del cuore."
(Family is the heartland of your heart). Italian Proverb

Luigi Amorebello - A Poem About The Life Of *My Paternal Grandfather*

The land was dry
The way was far
Louis was small
He rode astride
The shoulders of the men
Who daily walked the dusty road
To the sulfur mines beyond the hills
Of the village of San Cataldo
In the Province of Caltanissetta

Despite his stature small
Louis had a vision wide
As large as the great sea
That lay beyond San Cataldo
To school he went
He learned to read and write

A scholar priest, not miner
Was what his family dreamed
But neither was meant to be
Louis grew to manhood

It was in the village church
That Louis first saw his love
Behind a partition she prayed
With the other Sicilian girls
Because that was the way of life
In bygone days

He tore that divider down
So he could gaze
Upon the countenance
Of the one he was to love
For over sixty years
In a dream not yet realized

The army called
And Louis to Africa sailed
To become an army cook
In the land where the sirocco blows
So far from home

Calogera waited for Louis to return
And to the Western sky, they gazed
And stirrings of unrest and weariness
Set the couple in a new way

Louis could be a miner
And there were mines across the ocean
Mines with hard black rock
Where one could live a better life
And raise a family proud

Louis set sail in November 1907
With hopes so high
To the fabled city of New York
A younger brother reached New York
In the summer of 1907

But separate ways the brothers took
Which Louis could never reconcile
To the land of the Southern Cross
His brother went
And he was never seen again

Louis went inland from New York
To a place once called Bucktown
Near the woods of Dunmore, Pennsylvania
On the Lackawanna River

Louis worked the mines and lay down roots
In the shadow of the foothills of the Appalachians
Miles away from Manhattan Island
Far from Liberty Lady
And far from his wife and children

It was in the year 1908
When Calogera
And the children James and Louisa
Crossed the vast ocean
In the hold of an immigrant vessel
In the midst of hardship
In quest of a dream

The little family left their island

Bid the grieving relatives farewell

Wept one last time for the child Francesco

Forever asleep in his tiny grave

And saw for the very last time

All they had ever known

The crossing was rough

The space so small

The food was too little

Calogera paid for a piece of meat

But rancid it came

And in anger she threw it

At the man who felt no pity

For the plight of the travelers

At the mercy of Poseidon

The persistence of the winds

And the gods of the elements

But they weathered the journey

With only a breath of sea air

On the deck in the light of day

And then back to the hold

To steerage they went

To their narrow spaces

To the monotonous food

They clung to their dream
In the darkest of nights,
And rocked though they were
Either in calm or in storm
They held on so tight
To the visions they saw

Then on the horizon
At the earliest light
She arose from the sea
As the Goddess Athena
On the shores of Syracuse
Beckoning the storm-tossed
Calling as a siren to the weary seafarers
Who enraptured by her sight
Uttered never a word
But in silence watched
Their hearts swelling with awe

As the ancients of old
Beheld the Promised Land
That beckoned the wanderer
That pounded the inaudible words
Into mind and soul
"Here at last-you are here at last"

Louis with joy unimaginable
Took his family home
They wept for the lost island
That no one would ever see again

For home was no longer
In the dusty interior
Where Count Roger once reigned
In a Court that was regal
The land so rugged and dry
Their beloved families
Would be but a memory

Luigi Amoribello was born on May 31, 1875 to Vincenzo Amoribello and Luisa Cammarata in San Cataldo, Caltanissetta, Sicily, Italy. Grandfather died in Scranton, Pennsylvania on November 8, 1959. He had a stroke at home and passed away in the hospital. The immediate cause of death was respiratory arrest due to cerebrovascular accident and arteriosclerotic heart disease. He had anthracosilicosis (black lung disease) as a result of working in the coal mines.

I remembered Aunt Millie, holding his hand, leaning close, and saying, "Oh, Pa." He held so tightly to her hand as if by doing so, he could stay forever.

My grandfather never spoke to me. He was a silent man. I remember him lovingly giving a kiss with his bushy mustache, and laughing at my reaction to this. He wore the Sicilian coppola (the head covering of Sicilian peasantry copied from the fashion of the English gentleman) and took care of his garden and chickens.

My cousin Joseph A. Muracco remembered that coal was delivered on the front sidewalk. The family then chopped it into smaller pieces and stored it under the house. "All the children had jobs," said Joseph. He recalled sitting on Grandfather's lap in the backyard with the other Italian men, who were drinking wine. Joseph said, "Grandfather poured me some orange soda to drink." Grandfather was a kind and loving man from all accounts.

Grandfather's parents had several other children: Salvatore, born 1877; died Jan. 13, 1880, Angela, born 1880, died Nov.6, 1882, Angelo, born 1885; died March 18, 1900. The children that survived were Salvatore, born 1883; Giuseppa Maria born November 1, 1887, Cataldo born 1890, Carmela, born Oct. 14, 1893. Carmela married Calogero Amico. One of Grandfather's sisters was Maria (Amoribello) Cancilleri (Aunt Mary) who lived in Dunmore. Sandy Cancilleri was her son. Another of Luigi's sisters migrated from Sicily to Canada.

Grandfather worked in the sulfur mines in Sicily when he was about seven years old. (Did he want to go to school? Did he have dreams of America at this point? Where did the idea to emigrate first germinate?) The job of these little boys was to carry the sulfur ore to the surface from inside the mines. The children were called "carusi," and the miner with whom each boy worked was called a "picuneri" (pickman). The boys were sold to the miners for a few dollars; if the money could not be paid back to the miner, the boys were in servitude for a lifetime. The money to be paid back was known as a death benefit called the "succursudi murti."

The boys worked 8-10 hours a day and developed humps on their backs, lopsided bodies, distorted spine, and chest for those who worked their entire lives. They often developed pneumonia and tuberculosis. The boys did not survive beyond 25 years. Booker T. Washington on a trip to Sicily said, "It was the closest thing (the sulfur mines) to hell on earth." In 1902, a law was passed that did not allow children under thirteen years of age to work underground, and in 1905 raised the age to fifteen. The statute was not strictly enforced. Perhaps Angelo Amoribello (15 years old at death) labored in the mines.

Apparently, Grandfather's fee was repaid, as he was sent to school, and went as far as the eighth grade. My first cousin Joseph A. Muracco reported that the family wanted Grandfather to be a priest. Little is known about Grandfather's subsequent years.

Grandfather Luigi Amoribello (paternal grandfather) and
Calogera (Ingiamo) Amoribello (paternal grandmother)

The Amorebello Children: Left to right: James (Vincenzo), Louisa, Carmella (Millie), Concetta (Connie), Frank Salvatore (my father)

Grandfather and Grandmother Amorebello had the following children: Francesco (1903-1906), Vincenzo (James) (1900-1975), Louisa (1907-1963), Carmella (Millie) (1909-1989), Concetta (Connie) (1911-1972), Frank Salvatore (1914-1946), (father of Lucy and Charlotte), and Angela (1916-1916) who died in infancy in Dunmore, Pa. from premature birth. Angela lived about fifteen days.

Grandfather's army papers indicated that he listed his profession as "muratore" or mason. He was listed as single and could read and write. Dates of service were 1896-1898. He was sent to Africa. Italy had waged war with Ethiopia. The Italians were defeated in 1896. The Italians maintained a presence nonetheless in Eritrea, their only possession in Africa. Grandfather was engaged as a cook. (Grandfather's army papers were supplied to me by Joseph A. Muracco.)

The cover of Grandfather's papers says "The Royal Italian Army"; the "Personal Booklet of Luigi Amoribella." His parents were listed as Vincenzo and Luigia; Luigi's date of birth was 1875.

Italy was defeated in Ethiopia on March 1, 1896. Grandfather's army papers indicated an entrance date of March 8, 1896. If my translation is correct, Grandfather missed the last battle of the war (the decisive battle of Adowa) by one week. The papers are all in Italian, and the author employed an Italian-English translation book. The translation was like doing Latin in high school. To the best of my knowledge, a relatively accurate account has been interpreted and is as follows.

There were enormous casualties in the Battle of Adwa (Adowa) on both sides, but fate intervened for the descendants of Louis. He arrived in Africa after the disastrous battle.

Grandfather's army papers indicated he was an accurate marksman ("buono"). He was issued a rifle with bayonet, cartridge cases, shoulder strap, belt, and food provisions among other military supplies ("oggetti").

He became ill with "catarro" (excess of thick phlegm of mucus in the sinuses, throat, ears, or chest) and "bronghiole" (bronchitis) and was quarantined in the army hospital. The records noted he received bath towels, sheets, handkerchiefs, undershirts, ties, spoons, lunch boxes, and woolen bandages, underwear, pants, shoes, cups and plates, and gaiters ("uose") which are leggings worn to cover the ankle and lower leg. The date of his hospitalization is 1898, but I am not sure for how long he was required to remain under medical care.

In the first Italo-Abyssinian War, the Italians were defeated at Adowa (Adwa) on March 1, 1896. This was the greatest humiliation of Europeans by Africans since the era of Hannibal. The War came about because a rift occurred over the interpretation of the Peace Treaty of Wuchale in 1889.

In 1885 Italy garrisoned at Massawa. The Ethiopians found this an invasion of their access to the Seaport of Massawa.

The Italian Government was bent on colonization and Ethiopia seemed like a good prospect.

The Italians expanded into Eritrea, leading to skirmishes with the Ethiopians. During a fight, the Italians released balloons which terrified the retreating Ethiopians. However, on January 26, 1887, Italians were overrun in a narrow valley, leaving 430 dead and 82 wounded. This was known as "The Dogali Massacre."

The Peace Treaty (Wuchale) that was drawn up enraged the Ethiopians, as they felt it was misrepresented by the Italians. Supposedly, the Ethiopians believed they were now a sovereign country, whereas, Italy saw Ethiopia as an Italian Protectorate, under the governance of Italy. A war ensued, which was called the First Abyssian –Italo war of 1896.

By 1895, Italian forces were in Ethiopian territory. As of February, 1896, supplies were running low for both the Italians and the Ethiopians. The Italian General Oreste Baratieri recommended retreat, but his subordinates wanted to attack.

The Italian comprised four brigades of about 18,000 men (many of the soldiers were black Africans).

The Ethiopian forces under Menelik had over 100,000 troops. This overwhelming force was not known by the Italian Army.

The two armies clashed and on March 1, 1896 the Italians were defeated. Ethiopian troops armed with rifles, spears, swords, knives, 8600 horses, and 42 Russian artillery pieces routed the Italian army. The Italians had about 42 artillery pieces, inferior maps, old guns, bad communication equipment, and inferior boots for the rocky terrain. The Italians were tremendously outnumbered, and several gross military blunders were made by the Italian generals, one of which caused the Italian army to be divided and thus easily conquered.

Menelik, the Ethiopian leader, was a brilliant strategist, but Menelik's army suffered a loss of about 20,000 men out of 100,000 troops. There were 18,000 soldiers in the Italian army, 6,000 were killed. Some of the other men were either wounded or taken prisoner. Reportedly, the prisoners were well treated and in some cases befriended their captors. (Raymond Jonas *"The Battle of Adwa -African Victory in the Age of Empire"* 2011)

Italy signed the Treaty of Addis Ababa, in which Ethiopia was recognized as an independent nation. It was more than just a treaty. It was the only African nation that had defeated a European country, who wanted colonization of Ethiopia. Ethiopia was hailed as a hero in Africa and the African diaspora.

Africa was looked at in a new way. Black soldiers had won their independence. This became a pivotal victory for the rest of Africa.

When the Italian people received the news, there were riots in many of the cities of Italy. Prime Minister Crispi resigned. General Baratieri was judged as being unfit to command, and thus his military career was over.

Every year on March 1 Ethiopia celebrates this victory over the Italians, and more importantly, the defeat of colonization by a European power.

The Italians still retained Eritrea and troops remained. Since Grandfather would have been in Eritrea at this point, I speculate that he was the cook for these remaining garrisons.

The stories he could tell us of his experiences will never be known. To my knowledge, he never told any family members in Dunmore of his time in Africa. Grandfather belonged to the San Cataldo Club in Dunmore, Pa. The men who met there regularly may well have spoken to each other of events not known to their families.

It was reported by family members that Grandmother agreed to wait for Grandfather to return from Africa. What made them decide to leave Sicily is something that may never be known. Sicily was very poor. The land had been mismanaged, and there was a drought (serious lack of water) due to these faulty agricultural practices. The grapes failed due to a fungal blight (phylloxera). This destroyed the Italian wine industry. An aphid was responsible for the disease. This insect attacked the roots of the grape and laid its eggs in galls on the leaf.

The South of Italy had always been destitute. The industrial Northern Italy had always seen more prosperity. Sicily and southern Italy were heavily taxed. It was no surprise that southern Italians began a mass migration.

What exactly made Grandfather decide to leave for America in the fall of 1907 is not known. He probably sailed from Palermo to Naples to board the ship the Madonna in Naples. How he got from inland Caltanissetta to Palermo on the coast is also a mystery. In the Italian movie, *"Golden Door"* (2006,) the Sicilians are shown being carried in a horse-drawn cart to the seacoast.

I am wondering if this was the mode of transportation used, and how many others from the village decided to go at that time. Did the whole town turn out along with my Grandfather's immediate family, and follow the cart for awhile before it disappeared into the distance? It is interesting to speculate on just what happened on that momentous day. There must have been intense sadness because parents and relatives would most likely never be seen again. It had to be devastating.

When Grandfather arrived in Naples, the steam ship company performed a medical examination so that each passenger would not be refused because of some infirmity in New York. Otherwise, they (the steamship company) would have to pay the passage back.

Grandfather worked in the coal mines when he came to Dunmore. Cousin Joseph A. remembers Grandfather coming home from work all covered in soot from the mines. The Sprucks Coal Co. in Dunmore was Grandfather's place of employment.

U.S. Naturalization Records obtained through Ancestry.com indicated that Grandfather became a United States Citizen on September 7, 1916 in the Middle District of Pennsylvania. This must have been a glorious day for him.

Calogera Ingiamo Amoribello, my paternal grandmother, was born in San Cataldo, Sicily on October 14, 1876 to Frank Ingiamo and Carmella Diliberto. Grandmother died on May 11, 1971. Her death certificate indicated that the immediate cause of death was congestive heart failure due to generalized arteriosclerosis, and chronic brain syndrome. She was buried on May 15, 1971 at Mt. Carmel Cemetery, in Dunmore, Pa.

My sister Lucy (Amorebello) Jason reported that "Grandmother was taught to sew on a sewing machine at about six years of age." Little is known to me about her subsequent years in Sicily. She was versed in herbal remedies and folk medicine, most likely passed on from generation to generation.

Lucy noted that Grandmother was always concocting herbal medicines, sometimes boiling them on the stove. Lucy said, "Grandma, people are going to think you are a witch."

Grandmother also knew acupressure and would treat neighbors with various other techniques. Lucy said, "If a person had a headache and came to Grandmother, she would take the illness into her own body, and then sleep for hours."

To rid a child of intestinal worms, oil was first applied to the abdomen. Prayers were said. Grandmother then chanted in Italian, "cut one, cut two, and cut three." This chanting was to "cut" the worms from the stomach. The ritual was completed by making a sign of the cross over the patient. It is not known whether this remedy was successful. Round worms in people are treated today with mebendazole.

It is interesting to note that in the Sicilian movie, *"Golden Door," Director Emanuele Crialese, Miramax, Film (2006)* the grandmother performed an extraction of a "snake" from a girl's stomach. The grandmother loosely tied strings around the girl's body, and murmuring incantations in Italian, miraculously pulled the "snake" from the girl's abdomen, and all was well. The Sicilians were a very superstitious people at that time in history.

Grandmother's legs in later years lacked circulation and exhibited ulceration. Her doctor tried various things, but Grandmother had her cure. She used shaved soap and other ingredients to form a paste, which she rubbed on her legs every night and then applied a dressing. To her doctor's surprise, the ulceration subsided in a few weeks.

For treating venous ulcers today, the oral antibiotic pentoxifylline might be used. If cream is prescribed, it might be sulfasalazine or betadine. Surgical debridement might be indicated.

Lucy's children never had a tummy ache, as Grandmother made a drink of malva tea for them. She gathered the herbs in the back garden. According to the internet site *"Natural Healing Guide,"* the malva herb (Althea sylvestris) is pink to purple flower ubiquitous over the earth. Drinking the tea reduces stomach aches. It also helps with coughs and inflammation of the throat among other uses.

Grandmother also was a midwife; she worked with a local doctor. Lucy said to her, "Ma, if you had an education you would be dangerous." My grandmother was quite an accomplished woman for her time. She and Grandfather owned a grocery store near their home on Willow Street.

My grandparents entertained others from the old country in their living room on a weekly basis. Grandfather would read to the locals, and Grandmother would make her yellow cake with strawberry jelly on top. Perhaps Grandmother's sister Mrs. Alu was present at these gatherings.

When Grandfather was overextending the family budget by paying for others to come to America, Grandmother had to step in, visit Fidelity Bank, and stop any further payments.

My earliest memory of my grandparents was when I was six years old. My widowed mother and I came to visit. I remembered my grandparents laughing at some joke I told.

My grandmother was dressed in a black dress and wore black orthopedic shoes. She had very thick glasses, and her long white hair was always wound up in a bun. When Lucy washed and combed it, the white, silky hair reached the floor. She was always so happy to see me, and would smile and say "Charly." She spoke Italian, so I did not understand everything she said. She would admonish me and say, "Why don't you speak Italian?" Our parents did not seem to feel that was a priority. Those children, who did speak Italian, usually had a grandparent living with them.

There was only my widowed mother and I living in a small house. When I went to see my grandparents and extended family, it overwhelmed me. I remember visiting as a child and sitting down to a Sunday meal of homemade chicken soup. The house was warm and inviting, and the soup filled the kitchen with an enticing aroma.

My grandfather had on a starched white shirt, with a napkin tucked in at the neck. Somehow, even at that young age, I felt a sense of connectedness. Now I realized it was reminiscent of big family meals in Sicily. Perhaps it set the stage for my present quest of seeking roots.

Life was not always idyllic in Dunmore at Grandmother's house. There was a rift going on between Grandmother and another family reminiscent of the Hatfields and McCoys. The particulars are not known, but a bomb was set off in Grandmother's home. No one was injured, but Grandmother was incensed, and went for the gun, threatening to shoot the perpetrators. Grandfather, always the more passive spouse, talked my grandmother out of the plot. Grandmother was a rather determined feisty individual.

Research of old newspaper articles revealed that guns were openly carried, and duels occurred in Dunmore. An instance was a duel over a girl, Angelina Mecca (maybe a relation). Angelina was accidentally shot in the thigh while selling berries nearby. Her brother Charles was shot in the foot. The date of the incident was August, 1911.

Guns were commonly in the possession of the newly arrived immigrants. During the naturalization process they had to agree not to carry guns.

In my research of old newspapers via newpaper.com, it was uncovered that bombing of homes was sometimes carried out as a vendetta against the occupants. This was a surprise to me. For example, in March 1912 an explosion leveled and killed several people on Elm Street in Dunmore, Pa. A vendetta was suspected. The bombing of Grandmother's home was not a unique incident.

It was Grandmother who thought she could get work in New York City as a seamstress, and it was she who suggested they grow grapes and make wine in California. Grandfather who was more laid back wanted to stay in Dunmore and lead a more placid life. He was content.

I visited throughout the years, and always it was never enough for my dear grandmother. She would like to see more of me. As she neared the age of 95, she became bedridden. I remember visiting her the day she died. There were many neighbors there bidding my grandmother farewell. My grandmother was sitting in her bed, smiling, and she greeted me with the familiar, "Charly." "Why was she so happy and smiling?" I asked myself. I could not believe what I saw. She was joyous to go.

On an earlier date Lucy said, "Ma, you can't leave me." Grandmother said, "Lucy, I will stay five more days." Grandmother did just that. She fell into a deep sleep that afternoon. She breathed long, deep breaths, and I realized it was the finality of death. Later in the night, news came that Grandmother had died. I was grief-stricken, and now, as I write this, the realization has hit me that a generation was passing; a generation that ultimately brought us to the new world.

CHARLOTTE AMOREBELLO REMAKUS

A LETTER TO MY GRANDMOTHER CALOGERA

Dear Grandmother,
I remember your smile, your long white hair
Mounded and pinned atop your head
Your black dress so much the style then
I remember your greeting
A happy, resounding: "Charly, Charly, bene, bene."
It made me feel special
And loved, again and again

I remember the day
You called us to your bedside
And there you were, smiling, happy
And about to bid us a sad farewell
It was another journey, blessed
And you were eager for that voyage
Perhaps we all will meet on that foreign shore
Immigrants again and forever more

Thank you, Grandmother for coming to America
and giving us all a chance for a wonderful life.

"Charly"

CHAPTER 6 –

GRANDFATHER AND GRANDMOTHER AMOREBELLO'S CHILDREN

"Una buona mamma vale cento maestre"
(A good mother is worth a hundred teachers). **Italian proverb**

Uncle Jimmy was my father's older brother. He married Nellie Spinoza and they had three children: Charlotte DeCarlo, Antoinette Hnatko, and Louis Amorebello. Charlotte had two boys and one girl, Louis had three girls and one boy, ten grandchildren, and eight great-grandchildren. The surname Amorebella survives in New Jersey. Note that the spelling of "Amorebello" varied throughout the text. I wrote it as each family did.

Uncle Jimmy

James was my father's brother
The older of the two
I do not remember much of him
He married young and had a family
There always was a great big hug
And a few dollars in my hand
Now as I look back upon his face
Some memory of my father
Did I somehow discern?

Uncle Jimmy's son Louis Amorebella's Obituary from the Courier-Post, N.J. October 31, 2010:

"Louis P. Amorebella of Blenheim, N.J. passed away on Saturday, October 30, 2010. He was born in Lackawanna County, Pa. and was a Navy Veteran stationed on the USS

Bray. He worked over 50 years as a carpenter, mason and general contractor. Louis was married to the late Carmella (Parenti) Amorebella. Louis is survived by his four children Carmel Vogel, Patricia Coombe, Deborah Alexander and James Amorebella. Surviving are his grandchildren, Robert, Hugh Jr., Michele, Michael, Sharon, Tommy, Jimmy Jr., Tony and Nicky; and great grandchildren Dominique, Talia, Michael, Natalie, Riley, Giavanna, Jessica, and Johnny."

To this day, the surname Amorebella and family DNA thrive in New Jersey.

Aunt Millie and Aunt Louisa Amorebello

Aunt Louisa Amorebello was a healthy child until she began to have epileptic seizures at about five years of age. She was not able to attend school in Dunmore as the seizures became severely debilitating. The photo on the cover of my book shows her as a woman of about thirty-eight (she is the woman standing next to my grandmother). By c.1950, Louisa was completely bedridden and her seizures were accompanied by loud screaming. It was then that I knew her. At six years of age I was fearful of approaching her. My mother seemed to have no trouble conversing with her. Although Lousia tried to communicate, her speech was mostly unintelligible. She enjoyed my mother's visits. My mother had a knack for making people feel valued. A visiting nurse made regular rounds to assist in Louisa's care.

When my father was alive, he talked about sending Louisa to a private school where he thought she could get help. She remained abed for about ten years or so until she died.

Louisa

Louisa had come by ship when but a child
But ill-fated were the winds that blew
Across that wide dark sea
She had the malady of the gods
And of the great Caesar too
Her life was long but spent abed
A silent martyr and to a child
A very sobering sight
But my mother said
She was very bright
Despite her infirmity
She could count change
And knew if you came up short

She lived she died a forgotten soul
And my mother after seeing her
Said to me
"Your grandmother buried her in white."

Aunt Millie Amorebello married Peter Muracco and they had five children: Joseph (1930-1931), Concetta (b. 1928), Joseph Anthony (b. 1933), Louis (b. 1939), and Peter James (b. 1942). Economic opportunity brought the family to Philadelphia, where Millie and Peter spent their entire lives. I still remembered their brick homes on South Hicks Street where my two aunts and cousins lived. Sitting on the stoop (small set of stone stairs leading to the doorway of a home) on a summer evening was something special, as in Dunmore we had porches.

It was exciting visiting my cousins in Philadelphia. They always had interesting things to do. They were close in age to me, so I always had playmates.

Aunt Millie's home was always filled with music, and I can see the black grand piano that dominated the middle room. My cousins and their friends played their music all the time. Aunt Millie said, "The boys would stay overnight, and I would serve them food and beverages." It was a happy home and a joyous family.

Aunt Millie (Amorebello) Muracco on her wedding day

Front row left to right: Peter, Connie, and Louis Muracco

Back row left to right: Grandfather and Grandmother Amorebello, Joseph A. Muracco

Aunt Millie

I remember my Aunt Millie
Whom I loved from my early years
She always had a smile
And happy words for me
Gifts she brought, which
I still treasure dearly
Now sixty-five years later
I still keep ever near

A little doll in blue
And a scarab bracelet
It makes me remember
My beautiful Aunt so dear

Her childhood picture shows
Her hair of brown like mine
We would be known as Mora (Moors)
In Old San Cataldo Town

She told me she would have liked to visit
That Fair Isle
She shared with me
An ancient longing to know
Where was our ancestral home
So very long ago

Aunt Connie Amorebello was born in Dunmore. Uncle Julio was a next-door neighbor. She married Uncle Julio Juliano on July 4, 1935.They lived in Dunmore initially. Connie and Julio had a daughter Michelina (Micky) on 2/25/38. Eventually they moved to Philadelphia, Pa. where they raised their family. Their son Frank Juliano was born on 5/4/43.

Many lovely times were spent in Aunt Connie's home growing up: watching television with my cousin Frankie and going to the Mummer's Parade on New Year's Day. New Year's Eve on South Hicks Street was a busy affair. We all went out in the street at midnight and rang in the new year with all kinds of noisemakers. The residents of the street then opened their homes and offered food and drink to all that entered. The party was so different from our much quieter celebrations in Dunmore.

I do not remember this, but when we were about four, Frankie and I ran away from home in Philadelphia. A policeman found us and brought us back. My mother related this story, almost unbelievable, but true. Our parents were horrified.

Cousin Frankie Juliano was full of fun. Frank painted a beard on his face with red lipstick and called himself Abraham Lincoln. Aunt Connie and I could not stop laughing.

Frank and I looked so much alike as children people thought we were brother and sister.

Aunt Connie

Concetta was red-haired and fair
With eyes of emerald green
It would appear that Count Roger's reign
Did mark the family well
For Norman blood no doubt
Did indeed enrich
The native island soul

Not very tall, but a spirit loving
A nurse she thought she would be
But in those days, it was foolish thought
To have a lofty goal
A young woman's musings
Should better turn
To duties more mundane

A silver hairbrush was the offering
A token of a young man's love
It was the custom then
To seal an engagement
To further bless the match
Connie and Julio joined hands

In Dunmore they began
Later to Philadelphia
A new life to begin
Two children (Mickey and Frank)
Brought the couple joy
And life continued thus
But a darkening cloud appeared
Julio left Connie
And a part of her was gone

Although she asked the
Question why
Until her dying day
She did not falter on her way
She kept the children safe from harm
Although her heart was broken

I still can see the homey rooms
The flowered couch, the chairs, the table
I still can smell the food so good
Wafting through the rooms

She was a splendid person
I still can see her smile
She touched my life
And I will always love
The aunt with the Norman red hair

We lived with Aunt Connie in Philadelphia for a short while, as my father was dying of throat cancer at the Philadelphia Hospital (no longer in existence). Uncle Peter Muracco went to visit the day my father died. Frank was up that morning, in good spirits, and was in the bathroom shaving. But this brief respite was not to last. He died that very night. My mother said when I began crying that evening in bed, she knew my father died. My mother said, "Frank is dead." Father's one regret was, "I won't see my daughters grow up."

My father's final resting place was Mt. Carmel Cemetery on the O'Neill Highway in Dunmore, Pa. Because he was so young and well known as an insurance agent, the turnout for his funeral was enormous.

Wildwood, New Jersey (1950) left to right: Aunt Connie (Amorebello) Juliano, Mother Sarah (kneeling), The Author, Cousin Connie (Muracco) Mulle

Frank Salvatore Amorebello was my father. He was married before, but his wife Lucy died from septicemia following childbirth. I am lucky to have my sister, Lucy, from that first marriage. Lucy has two sons Victor and Frank. She has four grandchildren: Matthew, Adam, Danielle, and Lindsey. Lucy has a great-grandson Calvin. My father married my mother in 1943. I was born the following year. He became ill with throat cancer and died when I was two years old. My Mom had to support me, mostly by working in a dress factory. We tried living in the Bronx with my Aunt Marguerite, in Florida with my mother's godmother, and potentially in southern California. Mama was very young and searching for a new beginning. However, our roots always brought us back to Dunmore and the family.

My mother married Ted Wassel in 1954 when I was ten, and I am lucky to have my two sisters: Angela and Helen. Helen has three daughters: Ashley, Sierra, Tiffany, and one son David. Helen has three grandchildren: Hunter, Max, and Lilyanna. Angela has one son Martin.

I do not remember my father. My only glimpse of his life was through the stories of others. My sister Lucy remembered him helping her with her homework and taking her for Sunday afternoon rides in his car.

My mother said that he had a humorous side, and if he thought there might be an argument, he would throw his hat in the door first. On another occasion, he filled my mother's nylon stockings with coal and hung them on the fireplace at Christmas time. She threw his trousers high onto a ceiling light fixture so he could not reach them. My mother said he roared with laughter. I think they were in love.

My cousin Joseph A. said, "When we went for a ride in Uncle Frank's car, he would beep the horn every time I touched the glove compartment." "Uncle Frank would give me a nickel if I attended school," said Joseph.

My mother said, "We were taking a walk, and I said to your father, "It would be nice to grow old together." He replied, "What a very caring thing to say." Of course, it was never to be.

My father went to the Dunmore Public Schools, and then to St. Thomas College (now the University of Scranton).

Father was an English major and planned to be an English high school teacher. As there was nothing available in the education field, he became an insurance agent for Metropolitan Life Insurance Company in Scranton, Pa. Dad received a medal for outstanding service in the Insurance Company.

My mom, being the instigator of all things humorous, would leave amusing notes on his car windshield, if she saw his auto at a client's home.

Little is known to me about his early years. He became a barber to earn his way through college.

My mother said, "Your dad thought he got cancer from bumping his nose while swimming."

My grandfather Dominick felt he got osteosarcoma by a trauma to his arm. Grandfather mentioned this to his family upon receiving the devastating news. Aunt Anna said, "My father (Dominick) had his medical book open to the page of his diagnosis."

Cancer was at the areas of injury in both cases. Recent research indicated that bumps do not cause cancer, but that cancer happens to be at the site of impact.

Photographs are the only real evidence I have that my father existed and had a life although brief. There are also some written memories.

My sister Helen found this love note written to my mother by my dad:

"I love you dear, and you know that I do." "Forever and ever" Frank, Monday (3-22-43)

Frank and Sarah's Wedding 1943

CHAPTER 7 –

THE ITALIAN CONQUISTADOR

*"Mexicans descended from Aztecs, Peruvians from Incas,
and Argentines, from ships."* **Argentine Saying**

There is mystery surrounding Great-Uncle Salvatore Amorebello (1883-1918), who was Grandfather's younger brother. He arrived in New York in 1907. Nothing was known by the family in Dunmore regarding his whereabouts. It was thought he immigrated to South America. In the epilogue you will find the ending to this enigma surrounding Salvatore.

Salvatore

What a handsome man
I see
In a photograph so rare
A younger brother of my Grandfather
By eight years

An army uniform I discern
A cigar
A look of adventure in the eye
No restraints

A young man's fancy
Turned to the sea
But not to New York
A southern port he sought
Argentina was his goal

And then
The trail runs cold
What became
Of that brother
So bold
In a land
So distant from what he had known

Salvatore Amorebello

Salvatore Amorebello was a younger brother of my grandfather. He was born in 1883 in San Cataldo, Sicily. Nothing is known of his life except that he was in the Italian Army (at that time it was compulsory for every male to serve). This is corroborated by the uniform he is wearing in the only picture that I have. He arrived in New York City on July 14, 1907 on the ship Citta de Milano. He was 24 years old and single.

Grandfather arrived four months later on the Madonna. Reportedly Salvatore had already immigrated to Argentina. There is no definite record of this that could be found at the present time despite considerable research. The ship manifest for New York indicated that Salvatore did not have the funds to reach his final destination (Dunmore, Pa.). What happened next was not apparent.

Grandfather never spoke of this. He was not happy that his brother Salvatore decided on that course. My cousin Mickey Leonetti said, "My Aunt Millie wanted to go to Argentina to look for her uncle."

The records perused from Argentina showed no ship's manifest with the name of Salvatore Amorebello. There was a marriage recorded in Buenos Aires in 1913 and the father of the bride was named Salvatore Amorebello, but the dates do not match. It would mean my uncle Salvatore was only seven years old at the time of his daughter's birth (the bride) in 1890.

There was a second Salvatore Amorebello that arrived in New York a year earlier (1906) than my great uncle, and it is possible this man went to South America also. Since this Salvatore was 35 years and married when he arrived in New York, he would be the correct age for the South American father of the bride. All this was conjecture on my part. Oftentimes men went back and forth between Italy and South America to earn extra cash.

The trail ran cold for me, so I can only speculate what happened to this great uncle. He looks extremely confident in his photo, and appears to take great pride in his personal appearance down to the white detail of the shoes (it looks like white spats over his military shoes). His hair is meticulously combed, and he exudes almost a haughtiness and determination to fulfill an unknown destiny. He is wearing an army uniform, as all young men eighteen years of age had to join the army in Italy at the time. The cigar in his hand suggests he would like to be a man of the world and seek new experiences. I expect he would have turned many a young girl's eyes. But he had other things on his mind at the time. As a younger son, perhaps Salvatore was more independent, as is my younger son Matthew, who has moved 2000 miles away from the family home.

I will weave a fictitious story about a similar immigrant man named Francesco, including his bogus adventures and whereabouts. I speculated that Uncle Salvatore might have had similar experiences. I wanted to create a life for Great-Uncle Salvatore, the mystery man.

MY FICTIONAL ACCOUNT OF FRANCESCO

Francesco was intelligent and self- assured. He wanted the better things in life. He probably could read and write and felt little trepidation in leaving the poverty of his home. He was free as the wind and off to a great adventure.

He was congenial and made friends easily, and added much to the conversations on board ship. The passage was undoubtedly long, but he made the best of it. He maintained his impeccable grooming, was well liked by his fellow passengers, and kept them amused with his many daring stories. At a later date he might have become an entrepreneur.

Upon disembarkation and immigrant processing, he now found himself in a new world. Francesco was young and strong, and had an insatiable desire to make a home in this new hemisphere. He lived for the sheer joy of it.

The immigration to Argentina took place largely in the early 19th and 20th century. It consisted mainly of Italians and Spaniards, as well as Slavs, German, Irish, and French. Argentina had its greatest population growth at this time. The government promoted immigration as they wished to have the manpower to build a modern country. The immigrants added much to Argentina in terms of political beliefs, culture, and customs.

Most immigrants arrived through the port of Buenos Aires and stayed at the Immigrant's Hotel. The immigrant ate, slept, and received medical care, free of charge, for five days while securing work. Work began on the complex in 1906 and was completed in 1911.

Francesco came to Argentina in 1907 or 1908, so he would have stayed at the old facility known as La Rotonda de Retiro where the Retiro railway station now stands.

He watched the sun rise from the ocean as they neared the end of their voyage to Argentina. It appeared like a golden ball gently illuminating the early morning sky. Francesco became excited with the possibilities of this new beginning in a new world, far from the poverty and political unrest in Sicily.

A tinge of sadness crossed his mind as he thought of his parents. They had lost children who now lay buried. His leaving was another loss to them and equally profound. Although some immigrants returned to their homelands after the planting and harvesting season in Argentina as the seasons are reversed in the southern hemisphere, Francesco knew he was here to stay. He turned to a fellow passenger and said, "Do you think this day is a good omen for our landing?"

The man smiled and said, "I do think so." Francesco's adventure in this new land began as he made his way to the Rotonda de Retiro.

As Francesco carried his sparse bag of belongings, he heard a shout behind him. "Wait up friend." Francesco turned and a fellow shipmate by the name of Angelo caught up with him. They were to become lifelong friends.

Francesco might have had meals in a room at the immigrant's hotel. Facilities were opened at the new Immigrant Hotel in the order that they were needed. Food would be an essential element so I assumed the dining area would have been constructed early beginning 1906.

The food for breakfast consisted of coffee, fresh baked bread and mate (a caffeinated beverage made by heating the dried leaves of the yerba mate plant in very hot water). Reportedly it tastes like green tea. Sugar may be added for sweetness. Did Francesco enjoy this South American drink?

Lunch consisted of soup, meat stew, and pasta or rice. The children were given a snack at teatime (3pm). Women did domestic chores and the men sought employment at a nearby facility for that purpose.

Francesco and Angelo were grateful for the food and lodging that the Argentine government provided as they looked for work. When they found work they moved to a nearby tenement.

Angelo said, "Well, friend, what sort of labor should we seek?"

They had both done agricultural work, so they began as day laborers on a farm not too far from the city of Buenos Aires. They shared a room in La Boca, and looked forward to each day, as Argentina was a place very friendly to the Italian immigrants. They could easily assimilate, as the Spanish language, culture, religion, and food were very similar to what they knew. The Spanish language was very much like Italian, so acquiring this second language was not difficult. In addition, the latitude of the new country with the temperate climate made them feel as if they were home.

In 1816, Argentina was freed from Spanish rule. The country's population and culture were dominated mostly by immigrants from Spain and Italy from 1860 to 1930. The ethnic groups today are mostly white (Spanish and Italian 97%), and mestizo (mixed white and American Indian about 3%). Its terrain covers the Andes Mountains, glacial lakes, and the Pampas, where grain and beef are raised.

The indigenous people had been killed by the colonists in 19th century wars. In 1878-79 the remaining Indians were killed or driven to Patagonia.

The powers in control were the wealthy landowners. They began fencing in their estancias (ranches) and bred cattle and sheep. Each estancia had hundreds of thousands of acres. The gauchos (Spanish cowboys) began to disappear. The railroad came and opportunities opened. Immigrants were encouraged to come to help the country grow.

It was at this point that Francesco came to Argentina.

By 1912, there was unrest and the rich ruling group conceded to electoral reform. There was a secret ballot and all men could vote. Francesco would have been there at this change in the politics of Argentina.

The La Boca area was where Italian immigrants settled when they came to Argentina. Francesco and Angelo shared a room in a tenement in this area in 1908.

Francesco was strong and healthy, and he had an insatiable desire to make something of himself in this new hemisphere. There was no need to speculate on the past, as the past was dead to him. There would be no regrets. He wanted a better life than he could have had. Luckily for Francesco, he realized all of his dreams.

He and Angelo got jobs on a cattle ranch not too far from Buenos Aires. Francesco was a charming man, so it was no surprise that he met and eventually married Isabella, the beautiful daughter of a wealthy rancher. Isabella's father, Juan, owned an extensive cattle ranch and Juan saw much promise in the young Francesco. Juan blessed the nuptials of his only child, Isabella, and put Francesco in charge of the vast cattle ranch. More cattle were purchased and an expensive home was built on the pampas.

Francesco and Isabella became very prosperous. It was a love story, and they made a dashing couple in the rarified environment of wealthy landowners.

Two sons were born named Francesco Louis and Juan Emmanuelle. This was followed by two daughters Louisa Carmella and Lucia Isabella.

The family lived comfortably and continued to rise socially in Argentina society. "They lived happily ever after" was an apt description of the life of the former immigrant Francesco.

CHAPTER 8 – THE PARIS FAMILY

*"A mi la muerte me pela los diente." (Death peels my teeth,
which means Death can't do anything to me).* **Italian Saying**

"CHEESECAKE" AND PANCHO

Pancho Villa (1878-1923) was a Mexican revolutionary leader. He joined Francisco Madero's uprising against Mexican President Porfirio Diaz. The Mexican Revolution began in1910 when Diaz's regime was challenged. This dictator had been in power for 34 years, and many Mexicans felt it was an abuse of power.

Many of Pancho Villa's battles were fought on the northern border of Mexico. He became famous and Pancho even signed a contract with Hollywood in 1913 to have some of his battles filmed.

The U.S. initially supported Villa but President Woodrow Wilson moved his support to the new President Carranza, who was trying to establish a more democratic government.

As Pancho's military escapades began to wane, he entered the United States via Columbus, New Mexico on March 9, 1916 to obtain supplies, and to retaliate for the United States endorsement of the reigning Mexican President Carranza. Villa's army ravaged Columbus and killed nineteen people. Villa's crossing into the United States led to President Wilson's call for military intervention under the command of General John Pershing. Additional troops were required so eventually the National Guard from all the States were called for service. The U.S. army chased Villa all through Mexico but it was futile.

Although the army failed to capture Pancho, this foray into Mexico was a training ground for World War 1. The National Guard who patrolled the border from May 1916 to February 1917 saw little action but it provided necessary experience for these men prior to being deployed to Europe.

Although Pancho Villa eluded the American army during the Mexican Expedition, he was later assassinated in Mexico, when he again got into the political arena. Pancho said, "Don't let it end like this." "Tell them I said something."

Uncle "Cheesecake" (marked with arrow) during the Mexican Expedition
(1916-1917)

Francisco "Pancho" Villa (1877-1923) by Bain News Service Publisher.
Photographer is unknown. Public Domain via Wikimedia Commons (CC BY-SA 3.0),
also Library of Congress. Notice the bandolier across his chest.

Pvt. Anthony Towanda Paris (Uncle Cheesecake) joined the Mexican Expedition. He was a private in Company F, 13th Infantry Pennsylvania National Guard. He enlisted for State Service on Dec. 11, 1915 and was honorably discharged on June 8, 1917. Anthony's home station and point of rendezvous was Scranton, Pa. on June14, 1916. He was accepted into U.S. Service on 9/26/1916. Uncle's Mexican Service Medal was number 55B2. Cheesecake's enlistment expired on 12/10/1921.

According to the Mexican Border Campaign Veterans' Card File (digitalarchives.state.pa.us) (Mexican Emergency, Call of President June 18, 1916), Anthony was 32 years old, 5 ft. 6in. tall, had brown hair and eyes and was of fair complexion. He was single and his occupation was a laborer.

The infantry patrolled the border from California to Texas. The railroad transported the men to the Mexican Border from all parts of the U.S. The army was in search of Pancho Villa.

The world was on the brink of WWI. General Pershing and the army were recalled from the Mexican Campaign as the war in Europe was a more pressing issue.

Uncle Anthony's Draft Registration Card for WWI of 9/12/18 indicated that he lived at 208 Accommodation St. Dunmore, Pa. He was born on Feb.5, 1884. He was a carpenter for Bates and Rogers of New Cumberland, Rush, Pa. His mother Mrs. Sarah Paris was his nearest relative.

Mrs. Valeria Paris was instrumental in securing the flat granite marker for Uncle Anthony's grave, which is located at St. Catherine's Cemetery, Moscow, Pa.

We visited Uncle Anthony's home which was near St. Anthony's Church in Dunmore, Pa. He always had a houseful of dogs and cats and would encourage us to take at least one pet home. He loved his animals and always seemed like he was a happy man.

The Filippini Nuns who lived in the convent near St. Anthony's church tried to get him to attend mass. I do not think they were successful. He had his style.

It was rumored he was a ladies' man in his youth, but in his adult life he was married to Aunt Mary. Anna Mancia was Mary's daughter, and I spent many a weekend on Anna's farm in Hamlin, Pa. with her children June and Butch.

Going to Hamlin was like Paradise to me. I loved the open spaces and the earthy smell of the land, as well as the big old barn filled with fragrant hay.

I remember that Uncle Cheesecake babysat for me. He was a portly man with thinning white hair. Little did I know that he had been in both the Mexican campaign and WWI.

Today I wish I could listen to the stories he would be able to tell. There is a photo somewhere of him in the desert of New Mexico with a snake around his neck. He seemed to have an affinity for all animals. Perhaps my six cats, one dog, and two fish are a legacy to his memory.

My maternal Great-Grandparents, Peter and Serafina Paris, first lived in New York City where my grandmother Angela Maria Paris was born, according to my mother. I could not find a New York City birth certificate for my grandmother.

Great-Grandmother Serafina was born 02/08/1859 in Bella, Potenza, Basilicata, Italy and died 09/06/1934 in Dunmore, Pa. She arrived in America with Great- Grandfather Peter and her son Anthony Towanda Paris at Ellis Island on September 17, 1890. Marseilles, France, and Naples, Italy were the places of departure. The port of arrival was New York. The ship was the Neustria.

Serafina's father was Joseph Vitelli (b.1825) and her mother was Rosa Pentar (b. 1830). Great- Grandmother's parents lived in Bella, Potenza, Basilicata, Italy.

Great-Grandfather Peter was born on 07/18/1862 in Bella, Potenza, Basilicata. July 18 happened to be my son Chris' birthday as well.

Peter's father was Anthony Paris and Peter's mother was Angela Rispa. Great-Grandfather was a laborer. Great-Grandfather died on 2/16/1937 at 2 a.m. of cardiovascular and renal failure. Contributory factors were prostate hypertrophy with urine retention. He was 75 years old. He and Great-Grandmother Serafina were buried at St. Catherine's Cemetery in Moscow, Pa.

My Aunt Anna said, "Grandfather Peter loved wine, and Grandmother Serfina would dilute the wine with water."

Great-Grandmother Serafina was born in 1859 and died in 1934 at age seventy-five. The U.S. City Directories 1920 indicated Peter and Serafina were living at 228 Accommodation Street. Peter's occupation was a laborer.

There is little known about Great-Grandmother Serafina and Great-Grandfather Peter Paris. They lived a life unknown to me. They did help with my mother and her siblings Angelo, Anna, and Christine when Grandmother Angela Maria (Paris) Mecca died in 1925. Angela Maria had been their only daughter.

Mother remembered visiting Great-Grandmother Serafina who hid my mother's face as Great-Grandfather streaked naked from the bedroom. That is the only story ever told me about the great-grandparents. This incident must have left an impression on Mother.

The Paris and Mecca Families c.1925

Front row left to right: Aunt Anna, Cousin, my mother Sarah, Aunt Christine, Uncle Angelo Mecca

Back row left to right: Great-Grandmother Serafina Paris, Cousin, Great-Grandfather Peter Paris, Anthony ("Cheesecake") Paris, Cousin

This photo, probably taken by my maternal grandfather Dominick Mecca, appears to be at the gravesite of my maternal grandmother, Angela Maria (Paris) Mecca (1898-1925). Notice that Uncle Angelo (child far right) has soiled hands as he probably planted flowers

CHAPTER 9 – THE MECCA FAMILY

"Che sara, sara." (What will be, will be.) **Italian Saying**

The town of Avigliano, which is the ancestral town of the Mecca Family, is surrounded by mountains, some elevations as high as 4,000 ft. The average temperature is about 54 degrees F. The founding of Avigliano goes back to medieval times.

In the city of Potenza c.1149, Roger II of Sicily hosted King Louis VII of France, whom the Normans had freed from the Saracens. The city revolted against Spanish domination in 1694. They rioted again in 1848 and were repressed by Bourbon forces. Potenza rebelled for the last time in 1860. Then came the unification of Italy in 1861 of which they were a part.

The Mecca family grew grain and had a flour mill on a farm in Avigliano, Potenza, Basilicata, Italy. The farm is still in the Mecca family and my Aunt Marguerite (my mother's youngest sister) met with the relatives on a trip to Italy years ago. Due to my aunt's visit we were able to trace Great-Grandfather's lineage back to Great-Great-Great-Great Grandfather Sebastiano Mecca. There are no photos of this ancestor or of Great-Grandfather Angelo's father Vincenzo.

Below is a primary source of information from that visit. It may be of interest to the descendants of the Angelo Mecca family.

Sebastiano and Rosa Maria Mecca (b. before 1770) were my great-great-great-great grandparents. Angelo and Maria Mecca (b. before 1790) were my great-great-great grandparents.

Angelo and Maria Mecca had five sons (births in the early 1800s): Sebastiano, Antonio, Vincenzo (my great-great-grandfather), Giuseppe, and Vito.

Sebastiano married Maria and they had Incoronato, Angelo, Domenico (migrated to Montreal), Vito, Gelsomina, Donato, Carmela, and Assunta.

Antonio had Sebastiano, Angelo, Donato, Tella, Donatina, Maria, Donimico, and Salvatore.

Vincenzo (my great-great grandfather 1811-1883) had Angelo (my great-grandfather), Maria, Paolo, Gelsominio, Margarita, Geordino, Michelina, and Maria (who migrated to Caracas, Venezuela).

Giuseppe had Rosita, Antonio, Vito, Assunta, and Maria (who migrated to Montreal, Canada).

Vito (youngest in Rome) had Incoronado, Anna, and Donatina.

Most of the Mecca family remained in Italy. Some migrated to Venezuela and Canada as indicated in the previous paragraph.

There is a branch of the Mecca family in Caracas, Venezuela. My mother and sister Angela went to visit them with cousins Mamie and Anna from Sherwood Avenue. The Venezuela relatives owned a shoe factory and had a home in the city of Caracas, as well as a country retreat in the mountains. Some members of the Canadian Mecca family also visited at the same time.

My Aunt Christine and my mother took a bus trip to see the Mecca family that lived in Montreal, Canada. It was a very warm reunion of the descendants of the Avigliano-Mecca clan.

Some family members remain in contact with the Mecca families in Italy, Canada, and Venezuela.

Great-Grandfather Angelo Mecca was born January, 1847. He grew up on the family farm in Avigliano, Italy. He had a succession of wives, two of which died young. Angelo's second wife was Filomena Romano who died at age 24 (d.1868). I have no knowledge of his first wife. His third wife was Rosa Maria (Rinaldi) Mecca (died 1882). Vito Vincenzo Mecca and Mary Mecca were the two children from that union.

Angelo married Great-Grandmother Anna Maria (Mecca) Mecca in 1883. They had four children: Angelina, Josephine, William, and Grandfather Dominick John.

Great-Grandfather Angelo Mecca lived with his son Dominick John Mecca and family for a short time (U.S. 1920 census). When Angelo died in 1923 he was not living with Dominick. Angelo and his wife Anna Maria (Mecca) Mecca had lived with their son William and his family on Smith Street in Dunmore for most of their lives. William's wife Anna M. (Bonavoglia) Mecca took care of Angelo throughout his illness as he was eventually bed-ridden.

Great-Grandfather Angelo died in 1923. He was 76 years old. Great-Grandfather Angelo was buried with his wife Anna Maria (Mecca) Mecca at Dunmore Cemetery, Dunmore, Pa. His death certificate indicated he died of dysentery (duration one year) and myocardial degeneration (duration five years).

Vito Vincenzo (James) my grandfather Dominick's married half-brother came over first to America (c. 1892), and then sent for the rest of the family.

Family lore has it that Vito Vincenzo had an altercation with someone in Avigliano and made a hasty exit to America.

Vincenzo (James) married Carmella Rinaldi in 1891. They had seven living children out of nine pregnancies. Carmella's father was Vito Rinaldi and Angela Maria Carriero was Carmella's mother. Carmella was born in 1873 and died in 1930 of myocarditis and nephritis. I know nothing more of the family in ensuing years.

Vito Vincenzo (James) Mecca of 343 Smith St. Dunmore, Pa. died on April 29, 1927 of chronic myocarditis and uremic coma. He was 58 years old. He had been a night watchman for the Scranton Railway Co. Vito's father was Angelo Mecca and his mother was Rosa Maria (Rinaldi) Mecca. Informant was his half-brother William Mecca of 309 Smith Street. Vito Vincenzo was buried at St. Catherine's Cemetery, Moscow, Pa.

My grandfather's mother was Anna Maria Mecca. She was very strict. If you did not eat your meal, she would threaten to serve coal at the next sitting. My mother related this story to me. I wondered if this was a subliminal message for my mealtime habits.

Anna Maria Mecca (same maiden surname) was born in Italy in 1854. Her father was Vito Mecca and her mother was Angela Tolle. Anna Maria died on April 8, 1918 at 10a.m. from blood poisoning due to an infected wound in the palm of her left hand. The contributory factor was the lancing of a boil. The duration of the infection was 14 days. The death certificate was signed by R.J. Ritz MD. Great- Grandmother was buried on April 9, 1918 at Dunmore Cemetery, Dunmore, Pa.

Photos of Great-Grandmother Anna Maria Mecca (1854-1918) and Great-Grandfather Angelo Mecca (1847-1923). The photo of Great-Grandfather is courtesy of Christal Costanzo Occhipinti (4th cousin).

Great-Great-Great Grandparents: Maria (b. before 1790)
and Angelo Mecca (c.1789-1835)

My maternal grandfather Dominick John Mecca was a gifted man. He was born on September 11, 1895 and died on February 14, 1937 at 3:30 in the morning He was forty-two when he died. He was born wrapped in a caul, which he carried with him in a little leather bag throughout life, as a talisman for good luck. The en caul birth is when the baby is delivered completely encased in the amniotic sac. This is rare among births.

Although Grandfather started off as a "breaker boy" at seven years old, picking slate from coal, Dominick became a pharmacist and a respected member of the community.

Grandfather attended Dunmore Public Schools, worked as a grocery clerk, and as a life insurance agent. He later attended night classed at the Scranton Business College. He matriculated at St. Thomas University (now the University of Scranton) in 1916 and graduated in 1920. He went to Temple Pharmacy School in Philadelphia, Pa., and graduated two years later in 1922. Grandfather was awarded a gold medal at Temple for excellence in microscopy.

Grandfather Dominick would be proud to know that three of his great-grandchildren: Chris, Ali, and Matt Remakus graduated from Temple University Medical School.

Grandfather continued to work while at Temple University and was employed in a drug store in Philadelphia. Three months after graduation he became manager of that store. In 1922, Grandfather opened a drugstore in Dunmore, and in 1924 returned to Philadelphia to complete a postgraduate course in truss fitting. A truss is a surgical appliance to support a hernia. It is external and must be fitted properly for the patient's comfort.

Grandfather was a versatile man. In addition to his profession, he sang in the choir at St. Anthony's Church in Dunmore and the Jugger-Maennerchor Chorus at the Masonic Temple in Scranton. He performed as a soloist as well. Grandfather belonged to the Pennsylvania Pharmaceutical Association.

Grandfather also enjoyed camping in the woods and riding horses. He loved animals, and had dogs which he walked around Lake Scranton almost every day. Dominick had a great passion for music and grand opera.

Grandfather Dominick loved children and would enjoy giving chocolate to the youngsters, who came to the drugstore, and he became amused when the chocolate smeared their little faces.

On weekends he would take his children and the neighborhood children for Sunday rides in his car, a Pierce-Arrow.

The Pierce-Arrow was among the three luxury cars of the 1930s. It was made by the Pierce-Arrow Motor Car Company in Buffalo, New York. They supplied cars to the White House and to royalty of various countries. The cars were extremely well-made and reliable. During World War I, the Motor Company shipped trucks to Europe for use in the war effort.

Because of Grandfather's enjoyment of woods and country living, he and a partner Bill Mastracola built a vacation home in the Pocono Mountains, which they shared with family and friends. My earliest memory of that country place was a genuine black bear rug in front of the fireplace in the sparsely furnished living room. That bear met his demise on the front lawn of the Pocono home.

The backyard of this Pocono home was cool and woodsy and smelled of the mint herb which was growing in abundance. As I sat outside on that glorious summer afternoon, my mother walked into the backyard of the home and said, "Do you smell that fragrance?" She then said," It is the mint plant." To this day mint is my favorite herb and when I smell the earthiness of those leaves, it reminds me of my mother and that wonderful day in the Pocono Mountains.

Grandfather's young wife Angela Maria (Paris) Mecca died at age twenty-seven (1925) from pneumonia complicated by gallstones. The story is that she went out into a storm looking for her dog Fluffy. Shortly, thereafter, she and baby Christine Mecca became critically ill. The family feared there would be two deaths. Baby Christine recovered, but my maternal grandmother died. There were no antibiotics at that time and my grandfather, although knowledgeable in the therapeutic use of medication, was not able to save his wife. Grandfather was devastated. Reportedly he went camping to assuage his grief. The four children roamed the streets much to the dismay of family members.

My mother said "I remembered being lifted up to kiss my mother goodbye." My mother Sarah was four years old at the time. The children Angelo, Anna, Sarah and baby Christine lost what would have been a mother's deepest love.

Grandfather hired a housekeeper for the children. Four children must have stretched the woman to her limits.

My mother said, "The housekeeper tied me to the kitchen stove." It must have been the housekeeper's idea of a time-out.

Grandfather continued his work in the drugstore. He kept leeches in a barrel to extract blood from black and blue marks (standard of care in those days), was asked for medical advice by his clients, and made a proprietary cherry cough syrup which was found in the basement of his home as late as the 1960s.

Grandfather had fallen against his right arm in 1936 and felt this injury precipitated the onset of his bone cancer. His death certificate indicated that he was born on Sept. 11, 1895 and died on Feb. 14, 1937 at 3:25am. The principal cause of death was "injury to right shoulder and upper right arm which occurred at home on 8/18/1936." Surprisingly other contributory causes of importance were "sarcoma of proximal end of right humerus with metastases." It would appear that the cancer should be the principal cause of death. A biopsy was performed on 1/9/1937. At first it was thought to be a subdeltoid bursitis. There was no autopsy. The doctor was John Mecca, Grandfather's nephew.

Dr. John (Jack) Mecca died later in the year on April 7, 1937 of septicemia from a lanced boil on his hand. Dr. Jack had one son Dominick.

My mother said, "My father looked so sad one day." My mother inquired, "Daddy, why do you look so unhappy?" He died shortly thereafter when my mother was sixteen years of age.

As he lay dying, mother said, "My father suddenly sat upright in bed, looked mystically into the distance, smiled broadly, and then peacefully fell back on his pillow and expired."

All the businesses in Dunmore closed on the day of his funeral. My maternal Great-Grandfather, Peter Paris, said sadly, "Dominick morte." Peter's son-in-law Dominick was special to him.

My mother, as well as the rest of the family, felt a great sadness. My mother wrote on the back of one of grandfather's photographs, "Daddy, why did you leave us?"

In the early years of pharmacy, every drugstore had an ice-cream and soda fountain. The druggist was called "Doc" and at that point in time he served as a primary care physician.

Until the beginning of the 20th century, pharmacists were using natural sources such as foxglove for digitalis and made ointments, syrups, extracts, and teas from things of nature. My grandfather, for instance, made a cough syrup from honey, liquor, and lemon for coughs. Pharmacy was at that time an art.

In the 1920s, the manufacture of drugs had begun. Increasingly, drugs and medicines were bought from drug marketers. Pharmacy had become more scientific. By 1932, druggists were required to have a bachelor's degree.

Antibiotics take care of most pneumonia today. Children in the United States from birth to the age of eighteen receive vaccines currently for measles, mumps, rubella, varicella (chicken pox), diphtheria, tetanus, pertussis (whooping cough), hepatitis A, hepatitis B, polio, pneumococcal disease, and human papillomavirus (HPV) vaccine. The CDC (Centers For Disease Control) recommends meningococcal vaccination for all preteens and teens. A booster dose is recommended at age 16. If any persons are at increased risk to develop the infection, additional protocols are in place.

The influenza small scale epidemic in the 1930's might have been responsible for the deaths of little D.J. Mecca Jr. and eighteen- month old Joseph Muracco. This of course was not like the pandemic of 1918 when so many lives were lost to the Spanish Flu worldwide.

With the discovery of penicillin and other antibiotics in the 1940s, more people began to survive deadly illnesses. In 1951, Congress divided medications into prescription and over-the-counter through "The Food and Drug Act."

Grandfather would be amazed at the strides that have been made in medicine since he worked in his drugstore on Chestnut Street.

My mother kept this formulation for a rubbing alcohol compound for as long as can be remembered: 1 oz. wintergreen, one half oz. oil sassafras, one half oz. olive oil, 1 oz. chloroform, and 1oz. of gum camphor (John Sopho).

Grandfather's naturalization intention found on ancestry.com indicated that he was 18 years of age and worked as a shipping clerk. He was white with a dark complexion, 5ft. 4in. tall, and weighed 136 pounds. He had dark brown hair and brown eyes. Grandfather was living at 309 Smith St. He had sailed over from Naples and curiously he lists his last residence as Sterpito, Italy. The family originally lived on a farm in Avigliano; I have no knowledge of the Sterpito address. He foregoes any allegience to Victor Emmanuel lll of Italy (King of Italy), and is not an anarchist or polygamist. In good faith he plans to take up permanent residence in the United States. "So Help Me God."

Grandfather's enlistment papers for the army (WWI) indicated that he enlisted on April 29, 1918. He was 23 years of age. He was about 5'3" with dark complexion, brown eyes, and black hair. His occupation was listed as insurance agent. On April 30, 1921 he was discharged as his company CO C 2nd Infantry happened to be mustered out. He had no Federal service. Grandfather did not serve in WWII, but he belonged to the National Guard.

My maternal grandmother was Angela Maria (Paris) Mecca. Grandmother was born in New York City to Serafina and Peter Paris in 1898. Her brother was Uncle Cheesecake. My mother said, "She was a beautiful woman and all her clothes were exceptional in cut and quality."

Grandmother met my grandfather Dominick John Mecca in a store in Dunmore, where Grandfather was an employee. They were married early (c. 1914). Dominick was nineteen and Angela Maria was about sixteen. They had four children: Angelo, Anna, Sarah, and Christine.

My mother remembered my grandmother playing hide-and-seek with her four children. Grandmother said, "Here I come." "Where are you?" My mother three years of age responded, "Here I am."

My Aunt Anna remembered being a very talkative child at the dinner table, and Grandmother, a bit annoyed, hit her on the head with a pan. I am sure it was more symbolically.

Uncle Angelo remembered his mother pulling him out of a pool hall when he was about eight years old.

My grandmother died when she was 27 years old of pneumonia and was buried at St. Catherine's Cemetery in Moscow, Pa.

Grandmother Angela Maria Mecca (1898-1925)

Grandfather Dominick Mecca (1895-1937)

Great-Aunt Angelina Mecca, who was my grandfather's sister, settled at 407 Sherwood Avenue in Dunmore, Pa. Angelina married Peter Mecca (same last name) and they had the following children: two daughters who died in infancy, Lt. Salvatore (WW II), William, Donato (Tony), Angelo (Charlie), John (Jim), Lt. Col. Mike (WW II and Korea), Anna Shoemaker (Mike's twin), Mary, Peter Jr. and Angela. Peter Mecca (Hazelton) and his sister Angela McCarty (New York) survive.

I remembered visiting my Sherwood Avenue cousins in their home. They had a small garden with fruits and vegetables and some goats that were kept for milk. Chickens produced eggs for the family. They baked bread and made tomato sauce from their home-grown tomatoes. The neighbors complimented the Mecca family on the delicious aromas that emanated from my aunt's home.

According to my cousin Angelina (Mecca) McCarty, Aunt Angelina sat in her rocking chair every day to look at the photo of her three military sons, Salvatore, Michael, and Peter. She was so overcome with grief because of Salvatore's death that the family had to remove the photo from the wall. The family decided to have Salvatore buried in France because it would have been a severe emotional hardship to have his body shipped home.

On my last visit, when Great-Aunt Angelina was very old and bedridden, she looked at my progressing pregnancy and remarked with a smile on her caring, loving face, "A baby." Her daughters Anna and Mamie (Mary) cared for their mother in her declining years. Aunt Angelina once remarked, "Am I one-hundred-years old yet?"

My cousin, Peter Mecca, PhD. sent me the following primary source information regarding this family.

Lt. Salvatore Mecca, Anna (Mecca) Shoemaker, Mary, and Angela (Mecca) McCarty had no children.

William Mecca married Pearl Foglietta and they had one son William Donato Jr.

John (Jim) married Rose Koloras. They had four children: John, Rosanne, Pete and Sal (twins).

Donato (Tony) the oldest son married Esther and had two daughters: Chris and Penny.

Angelo (Charlie) married Frances Capozzi and had Rosemarie.

Mike married Ceil. They had one daughter Melanie. Melanie has a son Arden.

Peter married Catherine Coviello and had Peter Mecca PhD., Karen, and Melissa.

Peter Mecca PhD. married Donna Smith and they had two daughters: Katelyn and Angela. Peter Mecca is a biology teacher at a high school in Virginia.

One of the sons of Angelina, Lt. Salvatore Anthony Mecca was shot down over Normandy during World War II. A memorial with his name is in France near where his plane went down.

The memorial at St. Andre du Briouze is copyrighted so I cannot reproduce it. It can be found at www. aerosteles net/stelefr-briouze-mecca. The plaque is on the wall of the church of St. Andre de Briouze. It says: In memory of Lt. Salvatore Mecca, 10th photo Rec.GtP death 11.07.1944. At the bottom of the plaque is written in French, "US Air Force Morts pour notre LIBERTE" (Died for our Liberty).

His name and plot number in the Normandy American Cemetery is "Lt. Salvatore A. Mecca, Plot E, Row 3, Grave 33, Normandy American Cemetery, Saint Laurent, France." A photo of the cross taken by Frogman (volunteer at the cemetery) can be found at findagrave.com.

At the francecrashes39-45.net/page, you can see the information regarding the crash of the P-51 Mustang with the name "Heaven Can Wait." This was Salvatore Mecca's plane.

On July 11, 1944, Salvatore was on a photo reconnaissance flight from Chalgrove, Sussex, (southern England) UK to observe the movements of German troops, and the bombing of bridges. There were four squadrons. There was a heavy cloud cover. Four of the pilots, including Salvatore, were headed to La Violetieri, the target of the day. They encountered enemy aircraft.

In the combat that ensued, Salvatore's Mustang P51 (F 6) 43-12297 was shot down by German JG2 fighters (Fouk-Wulf 190As) and crashed at La Violetiere near the commune of Saint-Andre-de-Briouze at 1625 (4:25 pm). Jagdgeschwader 2 (JG2) was a fighter wing (military unit) in the Luftwaffe during World War II. Salvatore flew a reconnaissance plane. Salvatore was originally buried in the church cemetery at St. Andre de Briouze, and after the war, he was reinterred at Normandy American Cemetery.

Local townspeople rendered help to Salvatore, but he died of his wounds. There appears to be a discrepancy over the day he died. July 11, 1944 and July 15, 1944 are variably listed in different records as the date of his death. The rescuers brought a small box of articles found in the plane to the mayor of the town. At a later date, Sal's watch was retrieved that said "Mecca." Also salvaged was the propeller, motor of the plane, and the chassis that had inscribed, "Heaven Can Wait."

According to HonorStates.org, Salvatore's unit was 15th Squadron, 73rd Reconnaissance Group. His service # was 797872. His decorations were: The American Campaign Medal, World War 2 Victory Medal, and Air Medal with 4 Oak Leaf Clusters. There may have been other medals of which I am unaware.

The author retains a memorial page for Salvatore A. Mecca. This page can be accessed at findagrave.com. Add name Salvatore A. Mecca, Normandy American Cemetery in the search box. I have written a tribute. You can add a written tribute or leave virtual flowers.

There is a memorial to Lt. Salvatore A. Mecca and to all the veterans of WWI, WWII, the Korean Conflict, and Vietnam who lost their lives in war. The memorial is located in front of the Police Station on Blakely Street, Dunmore, Pa.

Salvatore's brother Lt. Col. Michael A. Mecca (1919-2007) was a veteran of World War II. He joined the Air Force. In Korea he was a rescue controller with the 5th Air Force. He and another pilot took 17 trips in a H5 helicopter to rescue men stranded in enemy territory. Mike received the Distinguished Flying Cross and received 11 other awards and medals. He is buried at Arlington National Cemetery. His wife is Ceil Mecca. Michael's daughter Melanie Mecca and grandson Arden Moscati live in Maryland.

My cousin Peter Mecca Ph.D. and wife visited France and saw the places mentioned regarding Sal. They viewed the remains of the plane and also were given a bullet retrieved from the fuselage.

So many young and beautiful people were lost during WWII. They sacrificed their youth and the chance for a future. While I was a child, peaceful and oblivious to worldly evil, all of this transpired. These heroes saved us. My tribute in haiku:

War

Crimson falls on snow

Summer sees the fallen son

Seasons all know death

I am proud of the members of my family who were the greatest generation. Aunt Anna and my Aunt Christine served in the Navy. Aunt Anna was a Navy nurse and Aunt Christine worked as a clerk in a naval store. Uncle Angelo Mecca (army) served in China.

Aunt Irene (Wassel) Mecca and Aunt Wanda (Wassel) Sanders were both Army nurses stationed overseas. Their brother and my step-father Thaddeus Jerome Wassel was in the Air Force and Merchant Marines, and served in the Philippines. All three of the military Wassels met during the war. The sibling reunion was highlighted in a news article.

My sister Angela said, "Dad (Merchant Marines) watched the torpedoes going past the ship." She also said he saw headhunters in New Guinea. Sister Helen noted that Dad was in Bora Bora.

In addition, my Uncle John Riggi and my Uncle Anthony Mercuri Sr. also served in the Army during World War II. Uncle Anthony, wounded seriously, dragged another soldier to safety. Aunt Anna said, "Tony's leg was laced up like a football."

Uncle D.J. Mecca Jr. served in the Navy during peacetime. He enjoyed being stationed in Bermuda. He saw a house painted in pastel blue and said, "A little house designed for two." He always referred to his wife Rosemary as "his bride."

Uncle D.J. had two daughters: Debbie (Mecca) McCauley and Yvonne (Mecca) Traficante. Debbie has two sons: Daniel and James. Yvonne has three sons: Frank, Andrew, and Mark.

I remembered that my Uncle Johnny Riggi said, "When I was in England, I never ran for the air raid shelters. I felt that if a bomb was going to get me, it was going to get me, no matter what."

Aunt Christine added, "He had a girlfriend named Christine when he was stationed in England." Uncle Johnny just laughed and said, "I had to ride a bicycle to her home to see her."

Uncle Angelo Mecca and Uncle Anthony Mercuri never shared any war stories with me. Most veterans are reluctant to talk about war experiences.

My mother saw Lt. Salvatore Mecca before he left for the war. He said, "Sarah, I see no future." My mother said she did not understand what he meant. Sal did not come home from the war. When my mother was dying of lung cancer she remarked, "Now I see what Sal meant when he said he saw no future."

Great-Aunt Josephine and her husband Dominick Mecca also had many children. They were: Anna (Mecca) Lepone, Jane, Lucy (Mecca) Ferraro, Dr. Jack, Monsignor

Mark, Charles, Dr. Donato, Joseph, James, and Dominick. None of these children survive at present. Those that I do remember were Jane, who was so sweet, Lucy, who was very close to our family and helped out whenever she could, especially when my mother was dying.

Cousin Lucy and her husband Armand Ferraro lived into their nineties. Lucy will be remembered always for her kindness. She had two sons A.J. and Mark Ferraro. They and their families currently live in Delaware. Many happy times were spent with our cousins A.J. and Mark when we were growing up.

Joseph taught school with me. My cousin Jane, saddened by Joseph's death, tearfully remarked, "I rocked my brother for his nap every day when he was a baby." Jane was a very loving and compassionate woman.

Dominick Mecca ("Minger") one of my babysitters took me to a bar (the old Willow Club on Chestnut St. Dunmore, Pa.) when I was four. I remember sitting on a barstool and watching television, which was very new at that time. I thought I was so grown-up.

Dr. Donato Mecca was my dentist. When I was in college, I tried to pull a tooth, and broke it at the base. Dr. Mecca was amused that I had been so innovative. When I was little, instead of using a drill, he carefully cleaned my teeth with a pick, as he knew I was afraid. It was interesting the things that you never forget.

Dr. Donato Mecca Sr. spent time in grandfather's pharmacy learning medicine. This was prior to Donato entering dental school.

His son Dr. Donato Mecca Jr. was our family doctor before he became an ophthalmologist. Cousin Donato had a dog named Skippy. He taught the dog many tricks. The one I remember was, "Skippy, it is Friday." At this point the dog would not eat his food. If Donato now said, "Skippy, it is Thursday," the dog would eat the food. This was so wonderful that we laughed and laughed at this trick. I was six years old at the time, but I never forgot the incident.

A younger son of Donato Sr., John Mecca, also became a physician and moved to Allentown, Pa. I became acquainted via ancestry.com with John's son, Doug Mecca, who provided me with information and photos for this book. Doug is a musician who lives in California; his band is "The Lucid Fly."

My only memory of Great-Aunt Josephine (Aunt Jessie) is that she dampened white bread and sprinkled sugar on it for me as a treat. I still remembered the sweet taste of the thick homemade bread on that warm, sunny summer day in her backyard on Walnut Street in Dunmore. Great-Aunt Josephine died on July 25, 1955 in Scranton, Pa. at the age of 70. She fell down the steps and broke a femur. She died five weeks later.

Grandfather remarried a few years later in 1928 to Marguerite Prisco, a beautiful woman from New York City. He met her through a friend Marie Telesca, with whom he sang in the church choir at St. Anthony's Church. Grandmother Marguerite had been raised in New York City. Her father had been a piano maker.

Grandmother Marguerite Grace Prisco had been working as a draper and designer, and was a gifted seamstress. She worked for Bonwit Teller, an exclusive women's dress shop in New York City.

Grandfather and Grandmother Marguerite had four children. The first girl was stillborn, and the first son (D.J. Jr.) died of pneumonia at eighteen months of age. My mother recalled that her father ran upstairs and downstairs to the pharmacy all night long in an effort to use every means to save his little son, who was ill with pneumonia, whooping cough, and suffered convulsions. It was futile, and again, as a healer, he failed to save yet another family member; Grandfather was heartbroken.

The Scranton Republican newspaper dated Jan.24, 1933 had the following obituary: "The funeral of D.J. Mecca Jr. was held on Saturday morning at the family home (Chestnut St.). A solemn high mass of requiem was celebrated at St. Anthony's church by the Rev. William A. Crotti, pastor. The flower carriers were: Leonard Carlucci, Joseph and James Mecca. Pallbearers were: Albert Prisco, James and Salvatore Mecca, and William Tedesco. Burial was at St. Catherine's Cemetery, Moscow, Pa."

Left to right: Uncle D.J., Aunt Marguerite, and
Grandmother Marguerite Grace (Prisco) Mecca

After Grandfather's death in 1937, Grandmother Marguerite, little Marguerite and D.J. Jr. (brother to baby D.J. who died in 1933) returned to the Bronx in New York City to be close to the Prisco family, and to receive their support during this trying time. We continued to be very close to our New York family in the years that followed. My Aunt Marguerite contributed a great deal of information to the family history.

Grandmother Marguerite Grace who died in her eighties was buried in the Mecca plot at St. Catherine's Cemetery, Moscow, Pa.

After the death of Grandfather, Uncle Angelo Mecca (1916-1993), my mother's older brother returned home to help care for the family. He had been at a Military School in North Carolina. My mother and Aunt Christine were under-age and there was talk of putting them in a home for orphans. Uncle Angelo, about twenty-two at the time said, "That is not going to happen." Both sets of grandparents were deceased, and the maternal aunts had huge families of their own. My mother 16 years old and Aunt Christine 14 years old were able to finish high school.

Aunt Christine said, "We rushed home from school at lunch hour to listen to the continuing soap opera on the radio."

Reportedly parties were hosted by these young people in the home on Chestnut Street. After all, there were no adults to supervise what was going on. My mother was friendly, loving, caring, and had a wonderful humorous side to her out-going personality. She loved people and showed it by cooking mounds of food for family and friends. Aunt Christine (Kiki) said, "Sarah's potato salad could feed an army." It does not surprise me that they entertained friends on a regular basis.

During WWII Uncle Angelo was stationed in Shanghai, China. I found a book of the Chinese language in our bookcase. I was impressed that my uncle was learning to speak Chinese. I once viewed a photo of Uncle Angelo taken on a balcony in Shanghai. I do not know if he was involved in combat. After the war he was employed by trucking companies. My mother said, "Angelo is a man's man, and everyone likes him." Uncle Angelo said to me, "I wish I had listened to my father and gone to college, and possibly medical school." He was much loved and that is what really counts in my opinion.

Uncle Angelo married Emma Schwasta on July 13, 1937 and had two daughters: Beverly and Janice. Emma's parents were Emil Schwasta and Anna (Nash) Schwasta. Emma's parents were from Austria.

Beverly (Mecca) Lesh has a store in the Poconos (Lesh's Leather). Janice and her family live in Texas. Uncle Angelo became divorced and married his second wife Irene (Wassel) Mecca. Angelo and Irene had one son Angelo Joseph Jr. Angelo Jr. is a music teacher in Poughkeepsie, N.Y. He is noted for his acting skills and beautiful singing voice.

Uncle Angelo lived with my widowed mother and me from time to time. He was kind and generous and often brought me little gifts. One Christmas when I was six he bought me an electric train which I treasured through my teen years. He often included me on day trips with his daughters, which I always enjoyed. One day in particular he bought us "foot-long" hot dogs for lunch. I never ate one before and that happy day remained in my memory.

My mother said, "Since Uncle Angelo works nights do not wake him up during the day." I followed my mother's dictum to the letter, but sat quietly by his bed until he woke up, and then asked him to fix or do something for me. My mother related this story to others as she found it amusing.

When he died in his seventies I remember lingering at his coffin remembering all the wonderful, loving things about my dear Uncle Angelo. He is buried at Mother of Sorrows Cemetery, Greenfield Township, Pa.

Grieving the death of her father Dominick, Aunt Anna Mecca Mercuri Gallo (1918-2017) (my mother's oldest sister) returned to the family home. She took a leave of absence from her nursing studies at Bellevue Hospital in New York City. She returned later to her studies, and became a Navy nurse during World War II. She was commissioned a second lieutenant and was stationed in San Francisco at a Naval Hospital, and later at Bellevue in New York City.

Aunt Anna had an amusing story about her time at Bellevue in New York. A sailor was continually getting out of bed and walking around wherever he pleased, against orders. Aunt Anna took his pajama bottoms away in hopes of forcing him to remain abed. The clever sailor, not to be deterred, wrapped a sheet around his waist and continued his meanderings.

Aunt Anna married Dr. Anthony (Mac) Mercuri, a podiatrist, and had two sons, Dr. Anthony Jr. and Paul. Uncle Mac was a podiatrist and died unfortunately in his forties of meningitis. My cousin Anthony Jr. became a podiatrist and lives in the Scranton, Pa. area. Paul currently lives in New Mexico with his family. He is the senior electronic digital computer mechanic for Tobyhanna Army Depot.

Aunt Anna was very close to all the cousins growing up. She would visit us at Chapman Lake and enjoyed all family activities. Aunt Anna and I walked around Lake Scranton on a regular basis.

As she grew older, Tina, Helen, Angela, and I visited her frequently. She was alert and kept up with things even though she was 98 years old. She spent her days resting and watching her favorite shows on television. She died of old age just short of her 99th birthday. She was so loving and generous that she left an emptiness that can never be filled.

Aunt Christine (KiKi) Mecca Riggi (1923-2004), who was my mother's younger sister, missed home so much when she was in the navy that she came home every weekend from Washington, D.C. She worked as a clerk in a store while in the navy. My mother said, "When we took Aunt Christine to catch a bus back to Washington, D.C. at 5a.m. in the morning Aunt could not believe that so many people were awake at that hour."

Aunt Christine married John Riggi and had four children. Her second child (Sheila) was stillborn. This child is buried in the Mecca gravesite at St. Catherine's Cemetery in Moscow, Pa. Aunt Christine said to my mother, "I often thought about that baby."

Uncle Johnny and Aunt Christine are buried at Fairview Memorial Park, Elmhurst, Pennsylvania in The Veterans Garden of Honor. Her children, Kathy, Tina, and Johnny, and I were very close growing up and we spent much time together.

Kathy has a son Serhii and lives in Chicago with her husband Andrew Chrucky. Kathy taught at the International Academy of Design & Technology. She specialized in fashion design and merchandising courses. Tina is widowed and enjoys her membership in the Corvette Club. Johnny and his wife MaryAnne live in Maryland and enjoy boating on the nearby waterways.

Aunt Kiki was a fun aunt. She always had time to listen to you and your problems with her own version of solutions. She would take us on field trips and picnics in her old Hudson automobile.

She was always a virtuoso of pranks. Aunt Kiki sewed the sleeves of our jackets closed so that we could not get our arms through. Canned goods were put under the sheets in the beds, and sometimes the sheets were shorted, so that you could not straighten your legs. We enjoyed all her antics.

One cold winter night, she gathered firecrackers, had us pile into her car, and drove us to the cabin where her son John and his friends were camping. In the darkness we set off the firecrackers. They made such a racket. We laughed so hard when the boys came out peering into the darkness in consternation.

She surprised me one night at a drive-in theater, when she pushed my cousin John into the back seat, and then jumped in with her other children Kathy and Tina. I thought it was hilarious, but my date was not amused.

She was missed very much, as Aunt Kiki and my Uncle John and cousins had such a loving, fun-filled home. The home on Cherry St. in Dunmore, Pa. was central to our growing years.

Aunt Kiki's love of animals was endearing. I remembered one of her first dogs. He was a black cocker spaniel named Nero, and he lived on Chestnut Street in Dunmore with us. This was about the same time I had my first cat, "Stinky." Aunt Kiki had a yellow canary, a dog named "Poochie," and many other animals that she adored. She said she wanted to be a veterinarian. Aunt Kiki would have been a good pet doctor.

Aunt Marguerite was my mother's youngest sister. She married Thomas Gibbons and they had three children, Marguerite, Tommy, and Christine. Aunt Marguerite currently lives in Raleigh, North Carolina. Her grandchildren are Tommy, Nicole, Sara, and Christina. Christina is a champion soccer player.

When Aunt Marguerite came to visit, she brought sunshine with her. Her personality was out-going, kind, and generous. I never saw her without a smile.

Aunt Marguerite paid a lot of attention to me whenI was a child. She took me to the Bronx Zoo, Jones Beach, shopping, playgrounds, and to restaurants whenever I visited her home at her home on 144th Street in the Bronx, N.Y.

A few times she took me on her dates with boyfriends. They did not share the same enthusiasm as my Aunt Marguerite. As we were riding in the car, we would sing "On Top of Old Smokey." To this day I love that song.

Uncle Dominick John Mecca Jr. (1936-2014) had the looks of a movie star. Uncle D.J., as he was known, was kind and generous and went out of his way for others. I remembered when he picked me up at nursery school in the Bronx, New York.

The nursery school proved to be a short-lived experience. Aunt Marguerite was late picking me up one day because a person jumped in front of her subway. The no-nonsense nuns had me sit outside the school on a stoop to wait for my aunt. This incident terrified my mother, and we moved back to the safety of Dunmore.

Uncle D.J. finished high school and enlisted in the navy. One hot summer day, we went to visit him in Maryland where he was stationed.

He enjoyed roller skating and met Aunt Rosemary at the skating rink. They were both expert roller skaters. They later married and raised their family in Brooklyn.

Uncle D.J. loved my mother's pepper cookies. Every Christmas I would send him a box. Rumor has it that he ate most of them. He is sadly missed by all of us.

My mother, Sarah (1921-1981), was a phenomenal woman. She had such strength of character, and was kind and loving to everyone she met. She was my hero. She had learned some Italian, and at six years of age, I listened in awe to her conversation with the elderly Italian ladies, who hung around my paternal grandmother's home, wearing their old-world black dresses.

Mother had studied Italian in high school with her teacher Mrs. Mafulo, and Mother was quite proficient. She also loved chemistry and may have become a pharmacist if her father had lived. "Sarah, I am not asking you, I am telling you that I want you to be a pharmacist," her father once told her.

My Mother was beautiful and had a great sense of humor. She always looked on the bright side of life; she saw the silver lining in every adversity. When I was moody, she would say, "Smile Luigi" (this was a popular radio show at the time). She was always seeking new adventures and was instrumental in the many trips we took.

She worked too hard and gave so much. I wish I could have done more for her. I was devastated when she died at age sixty of lung cancer even though she was a non-smoker. Life was never the same. She was buried in the Mecca plot at St. Catherine's Cemetery in Moscow, Pa.

I wanted to be sure she was alright in the after-life and asked for a sign. Six months after her death while musing on her promise, the doorbell rang. No one was there. I waited, and the doorbell rang again. No visitor appeared. It may or may not have been my sign that she was okay, but in some way, I felt it was.

Periodically she appeared in dreams to give me advice and to spend time with me. I am sure others have had that same experience from loved ones that have passed.

Through My Mother's Eyes

The box lied unopened
The contents long forgot
She had gone away
A long eighteen years
My life had milestones wrought

I handled the items lovingly
Memories of love and caring and strife
A memory of a blithe and happy spirit
A sojourner in love with life

There was a pair of glasses
The lens speckled with bits of dust
Thoughts of a young woman flashed inside my mind
A woman so full of trust

I put on my mother's glasses
And tried to see so clear
The things she saw, the thoughts she thought
The life's stories she held so dear

Through the mists of years gone by
A mosaic of life arose
Sarah looked into her sweet mother's eyes
Then slept in sweet repose

She loved her dynamic father
She vowed she would never leave
But when he died, that path was closed
And Sarah long did grieve

Caring for a family did occupy her time
She always saw the silver lining
She always was so kind
She reached out to others without a thought
Her laughter was sincere
She saw the beauty in every day
And life she did hold dear

She was the sweetest mother
Her smile diminished sighs
The world was always full of promise
Through my mother's eyes

My cousin, Kathy Chrucky, wrote this beautiful memory about my mother. She composed this piece as how she thought I would write it:

"Family was very important to my mother. She made it a point to bring all of the family members together to celebrate holidays and birthdays. She shared this tradition with her sister Kiki by alternating homes for each holiday. She always prepared a feast of turkey, ham, veal cutlets, roast beef, spaghetti, meat balls, lasagna, sweet potatoes, mashed potatoes, salad, home-made apple pie, and her famous banana cake. At Christmas she added Italian pepper cookies. There was an abundance of food and laughter for all family members. An adult and kid's table were always set up and she was called "Zia" by her nieces and nephews. These family feasts established a loving creative, humorous connection between all members of the family. The Mecca cousins have maintained this close relationship to this day.

"My mother's pepper cookies and banana cake were always the hit of the meal. Family members have tried to recreate these sweets from my mother's recipe but have failed. Some made them too hard and Kathy's was a complete disaster covered in white mold, because they were stored in plastic. My version is the closest to the original taste and texture of my mother's pepper cookies. All look forward to these cookies during my holiday celebrations. All remember my mother lovingly with each bite of a pepper cookie.

"She was close to all of her siblings but shared a special bond with Aunt Kiki. Aunt Kiki asked my mother to be Kathy's Godmother. Kathy told me that Zia always remembered her birthday and made a banana cake especially for her. Every day my mother would call Aunt Kiki at 12 midnight. They would talk about soap operas, their children, and the events of the day. Aunt Kiki was so lost when my mother died that her daughter, Kathy, became the midnight caller to ease her grief. She never got over the death of her dearest sister, Sarah. The loving relationship that my mother had with her siblings has been passed down to all Mecca descendants.

"My mother loved animals and had many throughout her lifetime. She even owned and managed a petting zoo at Rocky Glen Park with her second husband, Ted Wassel. When the zoo closed, she adopted the capuchin monkey. She was the only person who could feed and handle the monkey, Bozo.

"She was an entrepreneur who owned a petting zoo and three soft ice cream stands during her lifetime. My cousin Kathy and I worked at the zoo and Dunmore ice cream stand with her. She was a strong hard-working woman, who was loved by all her customers."

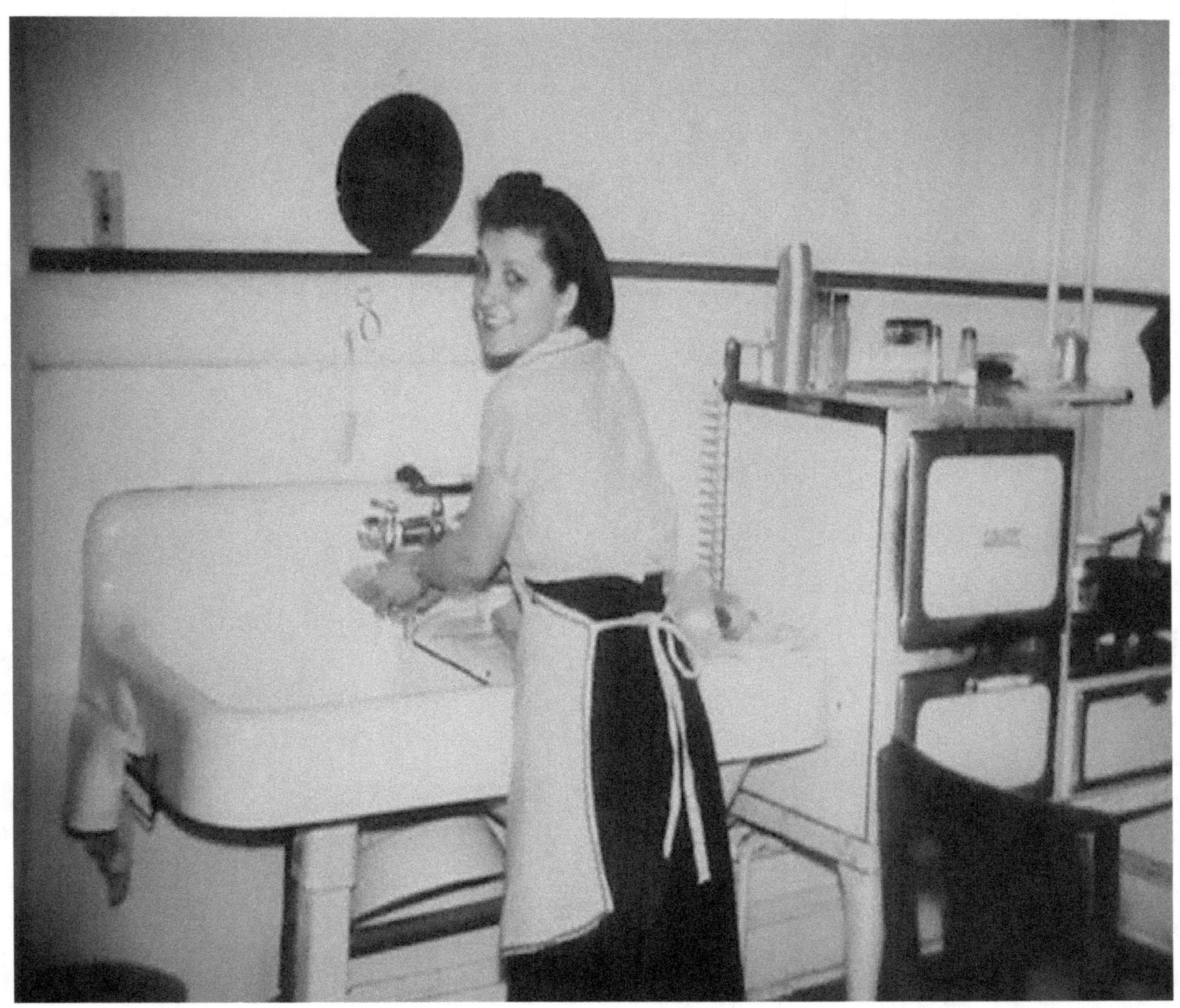

My Mother in her 1940's kitchen on Chestnut Street, Dunmore, Pa.

CHAPTER 10 – I, CALOGERA

"Know Thyself." Socrates

"By Nature, men are nearly alike, by practice they get to be wide apart."
Confucius

I am more than I imagined. I could recount my ordinary suburban, small-town upbringing. I could catalog my youth, schooling, professional life, marriage, and children. Yes, I am all of those things, and all of us have our particular story. Our fingerprints are unique, formed from the wrinkling of our fingertips in the primordial amniotic fluid.

We are influenced by so very many things from our unique experiences, and interactions with others we meet along life's way. Our thoughts, our perceptions, the reading we have done, and the movies we watch, all impact us in various ways.

Most of us at a point in time look back upon our lives seeing the best and wishing we could have done it better. We are wiser for the journey, and hopefully happier, and even more willing to help others on their way.

But that is not the whole story. Current scientific theory supports the out of Africa movement for modern humans. We are all of African descent. Those ancestors that left Africa are all descended from the daughters of a woman who lived between 150, 000 and 200,000 years ago. Her DNA survived and had been passed on to the present day. She is known as Mitochondrial Eve.

Some Africans did not migrate from Africa but remained on the continent. Their DNA is different from ours in many respects. Those that did come out from Africa carried the mitochondrial DNA from the original Eve and populated the entire earth.

Although this is the current theory, there are those scientists that support the multiregional explanation of the rise of different racial groups. They believe that modern man arose from distant ancestors in various parts of the planet, and not from one woman in Africa.

The aboriginals of Australia and the Chinese believe that they had an ancestor that arose in Australia and China respectively, and therefore they are unique. They do not believe that they are descended from mitochondrial Eve.

However, recent DNA studies have shown that both the aboriginals of Australia and the Chinese people carry the same genetic marker as the rest of us whose ancestors left Africa some 50,000 t0 70,000 years ago. This research puts the origin of our species directly in Africa. Over the millennia, we have adapted to various climates and cultures, and that is why there is so much diversity in the world today.

Why did this migration take place? Was there the scarcity of food which prompted the move from the African continent, or man's incredible curiosity of what lies just beyond?

These early explorers followed a route which skirted southward all the way to the subcontinent of India and surprisingly ended up in Australia. These people were the earliest group, known as haplogroup U or "Ulla."

That the earliest humans first migrated to Australia, following a southern route out of Africa was a surprising find.

There are no archeological remains for this as the sea levels were lower when these people made their way to Australia and now are lost when the sea levels rose again.

The second group, also haplogroup U, who left Africa 10,000 years later than the first, crossed the Red Sea and the Arabian Peninsula, eventually going northward to the refugium (area below glacial expansion). *(Wells, Spencer. (2016/12/4) "The Journey of Man: An Odyssey," http://www.youtube.com>watch)*

When the Ice Age descended, this group returned to Africa and then spread eastward to the Mediterranean region. This trek was haplogroup (U6) to which my family belongs. My maternal ancestors followed this route. U6 is the haplogroup to which my great-great grandmother Rosa Pentar, my great-grandmother Serafina (Vitelli) Paris and my grandmother Angela Maria (Paris) Mecca belonged. Our Paris family members are descended from these three women Rosa Pentar, Serafina Vitelli, Angela Paris, and Angela's daughters Anna, Sarah, Christine, as well as Sarah and Christine's daughters: Charlotte (author), Kathy, Christine, Helen, and Angela.

My daughter Alexandra and her daughters Betsy and Charlie belong to the U6 maternal group.

Helen's daughters Ashley, Sierra, and Tiffany are part of the U6 mtDNA, as well as Sierra's daughter Lilyanna.

Although males also possess the mtDNA of their mothers, only the female descendants of these women can pass on mtDNA. The men from the Paris family also belong to the U6 group.

Brian Sykes *("The Seven Daughters of Eve: The Science That Reveals Our Genetic Ancestry" May 2002)* gave female names to the seven haplogroups of Europe. "A haplogroup is defined as a genetic population of people who share a common ancestor on the patrilineal or matrilineal line. Haplogroups are assigned letters of the alphabet, with refinements that consist of additional number and letter combinations." *January 1, 2016 (isogg.org>wiki>Haplogroup)* These seven major groups according to Sykes are U, H, J, X, V, T, and K.

Sykes's book provided detailed information on the seven groups with the names, Ursula, Helena, Jasmine, Xenia, Velda, Tara, and Katrina with accompanying stories of how these people lived based on climatic and other studies of the era. These seven have ages between 45,000 and 10,000 years. Agriculture began about 10,000 years ago.

Mr. Sykes said "Ursula was the mother of haplogroup U. She lived at a time that was much colder than today. She was probably born in a cave in Greece. Her people were hunter-gatherers and would have come into contact with Neanderthals. Neanderthals were not primitive brutes as previously thought. These human cousins were much more civilized. They bred with Ursula's people. They are not quite extinct because today some of us carry up to 3% of their DNA.

Ursula's family tools were flint knives and scrapers. Ursula's ancestors had moved from the Near East through Turkey."

Haplogroup U was the first to take over Europe. 11% of modern Europeans are direct maternal descendants of Ursula or Ulla. These people came from all over Europe and had some roots in Scandinavia. These studies corroborate the findings of Spencer Wells (geneticist for National Geographic) and other researchers.

Spencer Wells in his book *"Deep Ancestry"* (Wells, Spencer *"Deep Ancestry: Inside the Genographic Project"* National Geographic, 20/Mar/2007) gives the following breakdown: Ancestral line: Eve>L1>LO>L2>L3>N>R>U>U6. Dr. Wells said this group is about 50,000 years old. Some U6 went north to Scandinavia, and another to the west along the Mediterranean coast. Today they are found mainly in North Africa.

After the last Ice Age, U6 ancestors went across the waters of Gibraltar, where these lineages are found in Western Europe, Spain, and France.

Wells said "These people constructed huts, and used advanced tools of bone, stone, and ivory. They made jewelry, carvings, and rock paintings. They were an advanced culture."

According to Spencer Wells (geneticist), Homo sapiens were an endangered species 60,000 years ago with the possibility of extinction. We numbered only about two thousand individuals. Today our numbers are in the billions.

Much had happened in the intervening years since 1953 when Watson and Crick discovered the double helix DNA or deoxyribonucleic acid. It consisted of four base pairs: adenine, thymine, guanine, and cytosine. The whole molecule supported by a sugar-phosphate base.

Current scientific theory supports the out of Africa movement for modern humans. We are all of the African descent. Those ancestors that left Africa are all descended from the daughters of a woman who lived between 150, 000 and 200,000 years ago. Those that remained in Africa are also of her descent. Eve's mtDNA survived and has been passed on to the present day.

She is known as Mitochondrial Eve (not Biblical Eve). There were other women alive at the same time, but their mtDNA did not survive for whatever reason. The population was much smaller 20,000 years ago, maybe 10,000 people, so there were fewer women around. Some women died, some produced only sons, and some female babies did not survive.

Some Africans did not migrate out of Africa but remained on the continent. Their genomes are different from ours in many respects. There is more diversity of DNA in Africa than those who can trace their lineage to the daughters of mitochondrial Eve. Those that did come out from Africa to populate the rest of the world carried less diversification, as there were fewer people in this small group (estimates are about 250 people). The gene pool was much smaller.

Although this is the current theory, there are those scientists that support the multiregional explanation of the rise of different racial groups. They believe that modern man arose from distant ancestors in various parts of the planet, and not from one woman in Africa.

There were early attempts by Homo sapiens out of Africa, but these nomads did not survive. Their fossilized remains dating 100,000 years ago are found in the Quafzeh and Skuhl caves.

There were two successful exits from Africa *(Spencer Wells, 'Deep Ancestry.)*" The first migration was across the Red Sea to the Arabian Peninsula along the southern route of India and onto Australia, which occurred about 50,000 to 60,000 years ago. These people went on to populate the Pacific Islands.

The second migration (about 40,000 years ago) was across the Red Sea to the Arabian Peninsula and then an inland route through the Middle East. This group (including my U6 group) went on to populate the entire world.

The branching of this second group eventually populated all of Eurasia and the Americas. We can trace this route using the mtDNA from mitochondrial Eve, who lived in Africa between 150,000-200,000 years ago. Those who never migrated from Africa have a much more diversified genome than those who left Africa. These native Africans do not have the same markers (mutations) we have.

However newer research suggested that there was a return to Africa from the Mid-East, and European genes have been found in some African populations.

Ursula was the clan mother of haplogroup U. To be such a mother you must have at least two daughters, to be able to trace the generations back to the original mother. I cannot be a clan mother as I have only one daughter. My daughter had two daughters, so she qualifies, as does my sister Helen, who had three daughters. My sister Angela and my sister Lucy cannot be clan mothers because they had only sons. Angela and Lucy passed mtDNA to their boys, but male progeny cannot pass it on to their offspring.

I received my Family Tree mtDNA on March 10, 2015. My haplogroup and those of my female cousins on the Angela Maria Paris side is U6a3a1. There are three regions (HVR1, HVR2, and Coding Region) that show polymorphisms or mutations at various places on the chromosomes.

Polymorphisms mean a change in pattern, not an aberration in this case. Comparing these mutations to others, who have been tested, genealogical relationships can be established.

I consulted Eupedia.com Genetics and found the following information regarding my haplogroup U6 and its subclade U6a3a1. It is estimated that U6a (the oldest and largest to which my family belongs) arose between 35,000 and 45,000 years ago during the Early Upper Paleolithic, but before the Last Glacial Maximum (LGM).

Ua3a1 has been found in low frequencies as far north as the Baltic, Finland, and the Maghreb (region of North Africa bordering the Mediterranean Sea), and Iberia, which accounts for my being matched to genealogically related people in both the Mediterranean areas and Finland.

The fact that the subclade (Ua3a1) exists in Finland surprised me at first, but now it is quite clear. Matches from this area have been sent to me via FamilyTree.com.

This particular group (U6) is found in the northern half of Africa, the Middle East and most of southern and western Europe. It is found at 2% in Cyprus, 1% in Syria, Jordan, and Spain.

In Iberia, it is 8.5%, 7% northern Portugal, 4% in central Spain. The highest amounts outside Iberia are in south-west France 1.4%, Tuscany 0.6%, Sicily 0.5 %, and southern Italy 0.5 %.

Rollins et al. (2009) studied brain pH and mtDNA alleles. Alkaline brain pH (high pH) was found in haplogroups U and K. High pH adds protection against Parkinson's disease and psychiatric disorders including schizophrenia, bipolar disorder, and major depression.

Another study by the University of Manchester postulates that higher pH protects against strokes. People with higher brain pH tend to have higher IQs.

It was interesting that my daughter's DNA (23 and me) analysis showed less probability of our family getting Alzheimer or Parkinson disease.

Another study by the University of Manchester postulates that higher pH protects against strokes. People with higher brain pH tend to have higher IQs.

The T16189C mutation (which my lineage has) reduces metabolic efficiency. It has been linked to inherited thinness, thinness at birth, and increased body mass index.

Causes of Death in the Family

My paternal grandmother Calogera (Charlotte) lived to be 95 years and died of old age. My paternal grandfather (Louis) died of a stroke in his 80s.

My maternal grandmother Angela Maria (Paris) Mecca died at age 27 years of age from pneumonia which today is treated with antibiotics.

My maternal grandfather Dominick died of cancer at forty-two years. His father Angelo reportedly also succumbed to cancer in his seventies, although this disease was not listed on Great-Grandfather's death certificate.

My maternal great-grandmother (Serafina) died of cardiomyopathy but as an old woman.

My mother and my father died of cancer at relatively young ages.

Two of my Grandmother Charlotte Amorebello's children (James Amorebello and Millie (Amorebello) Muracco) died of cancer but in old age.

My mother's two brothers (Angelo and D.J. Mecca) died when they were over 75 years of age. Uncle D.J. had a history of heart disease. Uncle Angelo had a leg amputation due to gangrene and his health deteriorated after that.

One of mother's sisters (Aunt Christine) died of heart disease at 80 years of age. The oldest sister (Aunt Anna) died this summer at 98 years of old age.

Genetics has a great deal to do with our health and longevity. DNA and its application to medicine are the future, and it is here now. It can only get better perhaps eradicating illnesses.

The entire human genome was fully decoded by 2003. The genome was the blueprint for the creation of the human race. Some genes have been located, which could lead to therapies to correct devastating diseases.

The Medicine of tomorrow will rely heavily on an individual patient's genome. The risk factors for certain diseases will become transparent, and therapies for various illnesses will be tailored and pinpointed with greater accuracy.

In Pennsylvania currently, Geisinger (Geisinger Magazine Fall 2016) is offering enrollment in a research project for its current patients. It is called My Code. My Code analyzes the genome of individual patients and uses that information to tailor a program of care. By taking a small amount of blood from a person, researchers read the genes looking for mutations (changes) that may cause disease or in some cases prevent it.

The information goes into a database (privacy enabled) if no abnormalities are found to provide researchers with additional information.

If genetic change is found in any of the 76 genes studied, the results are sent to Geisinger, who then sends it to your doctor. You can meet with the Geisinger team to discuss results and possible treatments. The future holds such great promise for medical advancement.

If you are at risk for cancer, CancerIntercept Detect (pathway.com/genome) will analyze 96 somatic mutations that occur in nine specific cancer genes including breast, ovarian, lung, colorectal, melanoma, head, and neck, pancreatic, thyroid, prostate, and stomach. This test is for people who are at high risk for cancer.

Howard Jacob Ph.D., (the executive vice president for genomic medicine at Hudson Alpha Institute for Biotechnology) said, "There is a theoretical recognition that genomic medicine will become the norm in patient care. I hope that shortly, sequencing is so common, accepted, and obvious that no one remembers it not being the norm." (*Genome Magazine Fall 2016, Volume 3, Issue 03*)

My Ethnicity

My Ethnicity DNA from Ancestry reveals that I am Italy/Greece 76%, Iberian Peninsula (located on the southwestern tip of the European continent; includes the countries of Andorra, Portugal, Spain, and Gibraltar) 2%, Caucasus (region located at the border of Europe and Asia, between the Black and Caspian Seas) 17%, Middle East 4%, and 1% low confidence regions.

This finding is not surprising when you consider my ancestry is mainly southern Italy and Sicily, and my mtDNA (U6group) eventually ended in these areas.

It is interesting to note that one of my first cousins (father's side) who was also tested by Ancestry showed almost the identical profile. A first cousin on my mother's side has a similar combination, as does a niece, and a fourth cousin on the Mecca side.

I found it amusing that I am related to people in Finland with names like Jarvinen, Heikkinen, and Makinen.

I received my Family Tree mtDNA on March 10, 2015. My haplogroup and those of two of my sisters and female cousins on the Angela Maria Paris side is U6a3a1. There are three regions (HVR1, HVR2, and Coding Region) that show polymorphisms or mutations at various places on the chromosomes. By comparing these polymorphisms to others, who have been tested, genealogical relationships can be established.

The mtDNA is a piece of DNA that is not in the nucleus of the cell. It is in the cytoplasm of the cell. mtDNA is contained in the mitochondrion which has its membrane and DNA. It is circular rather than linear like nuclear DNA and is passed from a mother to her children. It does not replicate as does autosomal DNA. Only females can pass it on to their children.

mtDNA is why we can trace back thousands of years and see what paths our maternal ancestors took once they had left Africa. mtDNA changes very little over time.

CHAPTER 11 – FAMILY PHOTOGRAPHS

"Your Dad Frank Amorebello wrote this, and I have kept it since I was a kid."
Joseph Anthony Muracco

"Pictures record places and persons in such a manner as to give to them a lasting definite impression on the person who snapped them, or better still one might say that to each person present at the time the picture was taken, a certain train of thought is manifested, according to the particular situation of the person or group. To one the situation may be joyous; to another, it may be sad; to another, it may be ludicrous or droll. However, the important thing is this: every picture seems to record a now, and it is this desire to catch again those pleasant or otherwise feelings and thoughts that urge one to go over and over and over these pictures in the never to be lived again past."   Frank Amorebello, December 29, 1940

By viewing this assemblage of family photographs, I hope that for a moment the people and memories of bygone times come to life. These photos are my tribute to all, to the living and to the dead.

I hope the stories in my book give us a glimpse of our ancestors' existence if even for a brief time. May we all treasure our lives and honor those who have also had their entrances and exits.

Christine (Mecca) (1923-2004), Sarah (Mecca) (1921-1981) and Anna Mecca (1918-2017)

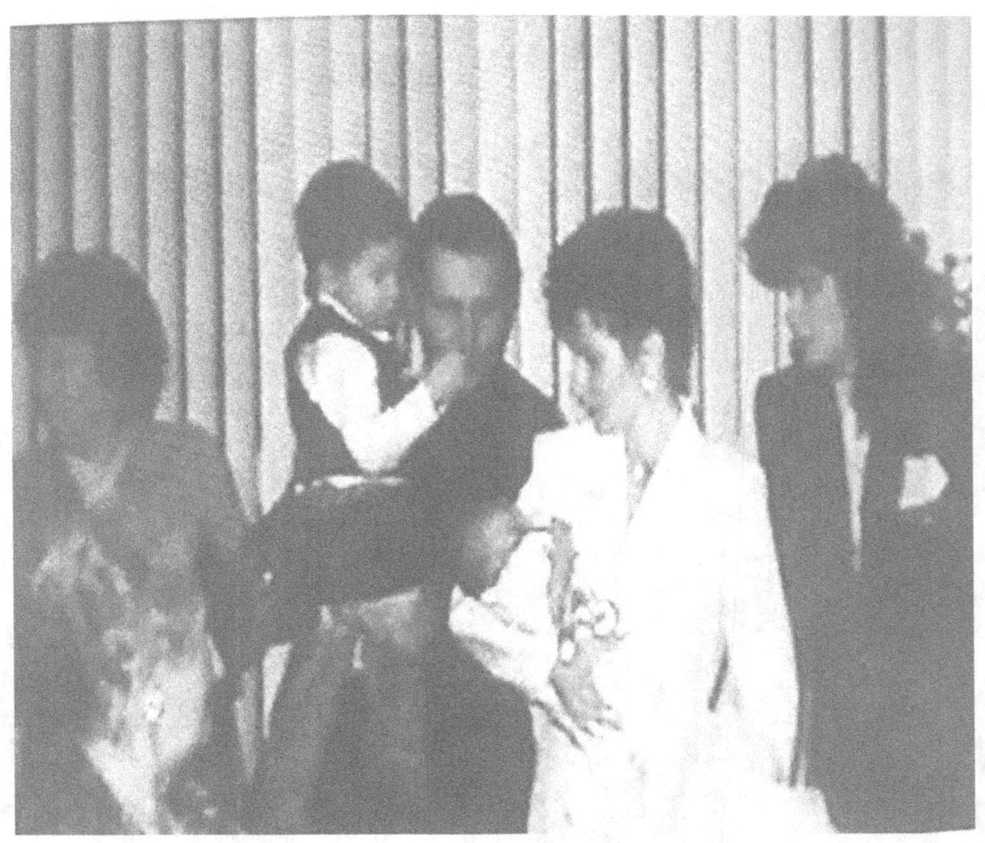

The D.J. Mecca Family: left to right Rose, Aunt Rosemary, Uncle D.J.,
Grandson, Yvonne and Baby, Debbie

The Novitsky Family left to right: Charlie, Dr. Ali, Dr. Mark, and Betsy

Drs. Matthew, Bernard, and Christopher Remakus

The Matthew Remakus Family: left to right Anabelle, Dr. Sanda, Jake, and Dr. Matthew

Drs. Chris Remakus, Ali Remakus Novitsky, and Matt Remakus

Left to right: Ashley Lancia, Hunter Lancia, Dan Hipsman, Dave Sartor and John Piv

Left to Right: Dr. Anthony, Anthony, Rachel and Katie Mercuri

Sarah Mercuri and Paul Mercuri, Sr.

Left to right: Dr. Mark Novitsky, Sr., Charlie Novitsky, Kathy Novitsky, Dr. Ali Novitsky, Dr. Mark Novitsky Jr., Betsy Novitsky, and Dr. Bern Remakus

Lindsey, Joanne, Frank, and Danielle Jason

Matthew, Lindsay, Sandy, Victor, and Adam Jason

MaryAnn and John Riggi   Tina (Riggi) Gittleman

Kathy, Andrew, and Serhii Chrucky

Sierra, Baby Lilyanna, Max, and Jamie Morano, Tiffany Lancia, and Martin Lambert

Doug Mecca (4th cousin) and Salvatore A. Mecca (2nd cousin)

Peter Mecca Sr. (2nd cousin) and Peter Mecca Jr. (3rd cousin)

The Author surrounded by her loving family:
son Chris, husband Bern, daughter Ali and son Matt –
a quarter-century ago

AMOREBELLO / MECCA FAMILY TREE

Vincenzo Amorebello 1776-1844
- Luigi Amorebello
- Angela Infantino

Luigi Amorebello 1875-1959

Louisa Cammarrata 1852
- Salvatore Cammarrata 1818-1893
- Luisa Pilato 1826-1900

Frank S. Amorebello 1914-1946

Francesco Ingiamo 1844-1911
- Ingiamo
- Mother

Charlotte Ingiamo 1877-1971

Carmela Diliberto 1852-
- Calogero Diliberto
- Calogera Monaco

Charlotte Remakus 1944-Living

Spouse
Bernard Remakus

Angelo Mecca 1847-1923
- Vincenzo Maria Mecca 1811-1883
- Carminella Colangelo

Children
Christopher
Alexandra
Matthew

Dominick John Mecca 1895-1937

Anna Maria Mecca 1854-1918
- Vito Mecca
- Angela Trotta

Sarah Mecca Amorebello 1921-1981

Peter Paris
- Anthony Paris
- Angela Rispa

Angela Maria Paris 1898-1925

Serafina Vitelli
- Guiseppe Vitelli
- Rosa Pentar

MOTHER'S FAVORITE RECIPES

ITALIAN PEPPER COOKIES   250-300 Cookies

5 lbs. Flour

1 lb. Lard, Crisco, or 2 cups of Olive Oil

4 cups Sugar

1 cup Powdered Cocoa

2 boxes Dark Raisins

2 Tbsp. Cinnamon

½ tsp. Nutmeg

1 tsp. Cloves

1 tsp. Salt

1 Tbsp. Black Pepper

2 Tbsp. Baking Powder

2 tsp. Baking Soda

4 oz. Whiskey

1 qt. Milk or Water

After mixing the ingredients well in a huge bowl, take small portions and roll into long cigars 1 ½" x 18" long.

Cut cigar rolls into a 1 ½" cookie.

Grease cookie pans and bake 20 minutes @ 400 degrees Fahrenheit for 15 minutes for the first batch.

Do not grease the pan again for the remaining batches, and bake each batch @ 400 degrees for 15 minutes.

Fill a water glass with Whiskey and drink at this time.

GLAZE:

1 box Powdered Sugar

8 oz. or more Milk

1 tsp. Vanilla

Mix the above ingredients together until the mixture is the consistency of a milk shake.

Dip each cookie in the glaze and set on wax paper to dry. This will take up a lot of counter space.

You may have to make the glaze a few times.

Finish the Bottle of Whiskey at this time.

Store the glazed cookies at room temperature just a few days, lightly covered. Then store in refrigerator or freezer for longer periods. Storing in tin or plastic bags for more than a day or two will cause mold.

BANANA CAKE

2 1/2 cups of sifted flour

1 2/3 cups of sugar

1 1/2 tsp. baking powder

1 1/2 tsp. baking soda

1 1/2 tsp. salt

2/3 cup soft shortening

2/3 cup buttermilk

1 1/4 cups of ripe mashed ripe bananas (about 3)

3 eggs

2/3 cup finely chopped nuts (optional)

Heat oven to 350 degrees F.
Grease and flour two pans (9x 1 ½ inches) or oblong pan (13" x 9 ½ by 2").
Blend flour, sugar, baking powder, baking soda, and salt.
Add shortening, half of buttermilk, and mashed bananas.
Beat two minutes at medium speed.
Scrape sides and bottom of bowl.
Add eggs and rest of buttermilk.
Beat two minutes scraping bowl frequently.
Fold in nuts and pour into pans.
Bake layers about 35 minutes.
Bake oblong 45-50 minutes and then cool.
Finish with butter icing or frost with whipped cream and decorate with sliced bananas.

EPILOGUE

This journey has taken more than three years. This meandering into the past all started with a visit to my mother's grave in 2014. Since then I have learned many things. Ancestor's histories have been made known through research involving many avenues of discovery. It is amazing that there is the wealth of material available to the average family historian.

Even more astonishing are the people I have met that are on similar journeys. Their stories and endeavors are inspiring, and have helped me in my research in ways that were unexpected.

We know we are here because of antecedents of long ago. Considering wars, disease, mortality, famine, and near extinction, it is a wonder we exist at all.

A fellow passenger on the QM2, whom I recently met said, "There appears to be at least one member of each family group that has an interest in the past and the progenitors of long ago." Thank goodness for that. Otherwise, all information would be so obscure in a far distant future as to be irretrievably lost. It is wonderful to have everything organized and researched for others who may have similar interests in family history.

This research has sparked my imagination. Many of the blanks have been filled in, but there is still much more to discover. Traveling to these enchanted places mentioned in the book and being immersed in the beauty awaits the modern explorer.

There is a desire to see all of Sicily (Palermo, Erice, Segesta, Agrigento, San Cataldo, Caltanissetta, Mt. Etna, Lake Pergusa, Taormina, Gela, Messina, and Syracuse) and in particular the places where my ancestors lived, loved, worked, dreamed, and died. There are museums and churches to visit, small towns, big towns, castles, Greek ruins, a volcano, ancient Syracuse, and the beautiful Mediterranean.

Avigliano, Potenza, Basilicata has been in memory for as long as I can remember. The name itself is mesmerizing and beautiful. To visit such a place would be the ultimate in family connectedness. Like salmon returning to their rivers of origin, it would be a spiritual homecoming. What feelings, what emotions, what wonder would be evoked in the on-looker? Then there would be all of Italy to explore. There is not time enough to be the recipient of all that is good and beautiful in our world.

South America looms in consciousness. My brief journey there has created a thirst for that mysterious continent. Once it only existed as a giant jigsaw piece on a map. Now it beckons like a magnet drawing me back to wonders only imagined.

Argentina was only a song I loved; the land where the gauchos (cowboys) lived. Now it is a place where an ancestor traveled and was swallowed up by that great, expansive, ever-changing country.

Salvatore Amorebello reportedly journeyed to Argentina in 1907. I was convinced he was at least a gaucho (Spanish cowboy). I envisioned him exploring and living in that country amid fantastic adventures.

Or was he?

There is an update on Salvatore. No record could be found of him in Argentina. Further research revealed that a Salvatore Amorebello, born 1883, parents Vincenzo and Luisa Amorebello, died in Sicily on September 16, 1918. Salvatore was married to Carmela Camilleri. They had three daughters, who died in infancy.

A third cousin Joseph Galletti (France) was found on familysearch.org, and he provided me with more information about Uncle Salvatore. Salvatore's first daughter Luigia was born in 1910 and died on March 5, 1911.The second daughter Luigia was born in 1912 and died June 1, 1912. The third child Salvatrice was born 1919 and died August 17, 1919. Salvatore died before this last daughter was born.

Joseph Galletti said that Salvatore worked in the sulfur mines in Sicily, and also was a farmer. Joseph noted that farming in Sicily was harsh at that time. My father Frank Amorebello was Joseph's second cousin once removed. Mr. Galletti is related to me on the Cammarata and Pilato side of the family; he is my third cousin.

The circumstances of Salvatore's death are unknown to me at present. The missing years are approximately 1907-1909.

The ship's manifest (Citta di Milano, 1907) indicated that Dunmore, Pa. was Salvatore's final destination. It also suggested that he did not have the financial means to reach Dunmore, Pa. He was able to read and write and was laborer. Where did he go? Where was he between the years 1907-1909? Did he go to Argentina, only to return quickly? Was he working somewhere in the States and then returned later to Sicily? No record of him exists in Dunmore, Pa.

I found an entry in Buffalo, New York, of a Salvatore Amorebello, laborer, who was living on Water Street in that city in 1907. Whether or not Salvatore worked there before returning to Sicily is speculative. It seems doubtful that he ever went to Argentina. Perhaps he will always be elusive.

Maybe when I visit Sicily, I can fill in the missing pieces.

To find the answers will require more research. It will be called "Finding Sal."

There was WWI going on in Europe which involved Italy. Italy had declared war on Austria-Hungary on May 23, 1915. By the time the war ended, in November 1918, 615,000 Italians had been killed. Salvatore died on September 16, 1918. Could he have fought in the war, and perished? Did he die of sickness; an accident?

Research often leaves many unanswered questions, which in turn requires more investigation. It is that which intrigues and advances knowledge.

This book has brought to mind the lives of those who preceded us. It only provides glimpses of the past. It has brought back to us our ancestors as living, breathing, real human beings, who had a chance at life (or not) and probably did not much wonder about who we would be in the ensuing years.

Our ancestors have been given a second chance to live on the pages of my book. What would they think of us in 2017, if they could come back and enjoy a day? I would invite them to my kitchen table for a meal, and all of us would be there. It would be quite an assemblage, and they would probably be overwhelmed.

They would look around and be amazed at all they had ultimately created. Smiles would crinkle their mouths as they beheld the beautiful little ones, and reach out their arms to encircle their great-great-great-great-great-great grandchildren. They would of course look for family resemblances, as every family does. They would, however, wonder who we were and how we came to be. We are largely unknown, but they ascertain that we are theirs. They would marvel at the modern conveniences and how vastly the world has changed.

Their eyes would twinkle with pride. How well our descendants have done. Our ancient families are pleased.

As they gaze at the babies, would they reach for them and perhaps sing them an ancient lullaby? Would they be happy with the clan they forged so long ago? Would they say, "Sangue Mio," (my blood)? They pour blessings on us in Italian. It is surreal to hear the ancient voices.

Perhaps they would arch their eyebrows at my crock pot spaghetti sauce, my store-bought pasta, and my bread-machine baked bread. They would shake their heads in dismay thinking their food was better. They would certainly recognize the Italian pepper cookies, the anise cookies, and the pasta I have prepared.

We look at them and take in their physical features, their demeanors, their faces, their speech, and their happiness of sharing time. They are glad to be here, albeit for a very short while. Who are these wonderful people that we never or only briefly knew? Their stories are lost in time

So much has been discovered in this endeavor. Being lost in the past has been mind-expanding. Much has been discovered, and this, in turn, required much thought and speculation.

This search has reunited me with cousins and other relatives and friends, who have provided information, insights, and photos to complete this book. I enjoyed reconnecting with people that were rarely seen or previously unknown.

There is a new appreciation of people in general as I realize all have their very own stories, and I am eager to listen. I have connected with people on the internet who share my passion. Findagrave.com enticed me to help others find their relatives' last resting places. This has been quite illuminating.

In the future volunteer work assisting others in their pursuit of relatives has become a very real possibility.

My interests have led me to become a member of the Dunmore Historical Society, Dunmore, Pa. This will lead me to even further adventures.

My DNA studies have illuminated how very much we are alike. It has made a rather shy person more out-going, as a result of this. It seemed most people enjoyed talking about where their families originated as well as telling family stories.

DNA studies have given me a different perspective on myself, as to who I am in this vast maze of life.

This endeavor has led to reading research in the discipline of genetics, the origin of man, and the miraculous spread of humans over the earth. Medical aspects of curing disease through genes intrigued me as to what the future may hold.

I have grown spiritually and mentally and have become enlightened as to how all of life is interconnected. I am stunned by the resiliency of the human race; I am saddened by the meanness on our earth; I am dedicated to making life better for all living things, and I admire those who work for peace and caring amid all the strife.

I enjoyed writing this book even though it took more than three years, and hours upon hours of research. It was well worth the effort. Now in one book is the history of our families to the best of my knowledge.

I am happy. My sojourn is complete.

ABOUT THE AUTHOR

Charlotte Amorebello Remakus was born on 7/14/44. Her early life was spent in Dunmore, Pa. and Simpson, Pa. She graduated from Marywood University, Scranton, Pa. with a teaching degree in Biological Science (B.S.), and a Masters Degree in Psychology with School Psychology Certification. She obtained a Master's Degree in Biological Science at East Stroudsburg University, Stroudsburg, Pa.

Currently, she teaches environmental science at Salt Springs State Park, Montrose, Pa. She lives in Hallstead, Pa. with her husband Dr. Bernard Remakus, her dog Chloe, and her six cats.

Charlotte is the proud mother of Dr. Christopher Remakus, Dr. Alexandra Novitsky, and Dr. Matthew Remakus.

Her great loves are her grandchildren: Jake and Anabelle Remakus, and Betsy and Charlie Novitsky.